MOVING WINDOWS

MOVING WINDOWS

Evaluating the Poetry Children Write

Jack Collom

Teachers & Writers Collaborative
New York, N.Y.

Moving Windows: Evaluating the Poetry Children Write

Funding for this publication has been provided by The New York State Council on the Arts.

Teachers & Writers Collaborative programs and publications are also made possible by funding from American Broadcasting Companies, Inc., American Stock Exchange, Chemical Bank, Consolidated Edison Company, General Electric Foundation, The Hugh M. Hefner Foundation, Mobil Foundation, Inc., Morgan Guaranty Trust Company, Morgan Stanley, New York Community Trust, New York Foundation for the Arts' Artists-in-Residence Program (supported by funds from the National Endowment for the Arts), New York Telephone, The New York Times Company Foundation, Henry Nias Foundation, Overseas Shipholding Group, Inc., Helena Rubinstein Foundation, The Scherman Foundation, and Variety Club.

Teachers and Writers Collaborative
5 Union Square West
New York, N.Y. 10003

Library of Congress Cataloging in Publication Data

Collom, Jack, 1931-
    Moving windows.

    1. Poetry—Study and teaching (Elementary)
2. Poetry—Study and teaching (Secondary)
3. School verse, American. I. Title.
PN1101.C66 1985   808.1'07'1073   85-9803
ISBN 0-915924-55-2

CONTENTS

PREFACE

Though I have worked in schools for years, I have never worked a day in a school without getting excited about some of the things the kids wrote. This book contains hundreds of examples of such writings (poems and prose poems). Generally speaking, however, children's poetry shows little sustained versification skill, precision of thought, conscious subtlety, or breadth of metaphoric reference. Lacking these possibilities for involvement (or distraction), the adult mind turns to and focuses on the tiny happenings in children's poetry, from word to word, musical, imagistic, ideational. The effect is a back-to-basics concentration that seems refreshingly simple and aesthetically solid.

Children tend to write works that contain wonderful flashes of poetry. They show little appetite for revision, and their writings are often lifelessly conventional or generalized. But they, being youthful, are "naturals." The descriptive word most often applied to children's art is "fresh." What does this mean? I think it means chiefly that, in lacking a sophisticated adult context of moral or other philosophical acceptability into which impressions must fit, the child is likely to get simple, direct, sensory takes on phenomena, and find words to match. The verbal juxtapositions may thereby be full of surprises, since they come more from an instant than a structure. However significant the elaborate adult skills are in poetry—and this is not to deny that significance—the spirit, the vivifying spark, remains surprise, which is proof of accuracy to the moment, of originality.

The bulk of the writings in this book have come from poetry workshops I've led in New York City schools since 1980. This has been a full-time occupation, and the number of works to choose from is vast. These poems are by kids from kindergarten through high school, mostly third-sixth graders. Some of the writings come from previous poetry-in-the-schools work in Colorado and Nebraska. Some come from my own children, mostly in the form of collaborations with me. My school residencies have usually been short; there's been little chance for long-term development.

I have tried to be inductive in composing this book, that is, to work from the children's writings "up." This tends to combat the inevitable tendency to impose one's own preconceptions on art material. I've tried not to organize the book so tightly as to make the poems seem to fall into place like eggs in a sorter. My method has been as follows.

I went through my collection of workshop poems (each residency in a school results in an anthology of the writing done) and circled my favorites. This was, by then, the third winnowing. I photocopied the entire mass, cut out the favorites and pasted them on legal-sized sheets, many crammed on each page, classifying each according to the type of writing exercise that evoked it. Then I jotted red-pen comments, attempting to note swiftly the essential quality of each poem and to point out the key details. From these comments emerged a set of qualities that seem to exist in children's poetry.

These qualities are roughly as follows:

• Candidness and innocence: The simple, unfettered realism children can have. The ability to see a thing as it is, not as it may fit one's world view. Children certainly have biases, but which tend to be transparent. Kids are also more capable of obvious contradiction, which helps in poetry, as Whitman let us know. These qualities lead not only to pure, simple "takes" on what's seen but also to revelations of the quirks of the human mind and to original use of language.

• Energy: Kids can often leap about rapidly in a richness of ideas and get this into their poems. Their verbal energy, once it's rolling, tends to be uninhibited. They also frequently invest their surroundings with a sense of life, speaking of even inanimate objects as if they had their own wills and spirits.

• Surprise: Partly because their thoughts are not routinized, kids are likely to respond to the newness of each detail, which allows the natural surprises of the world to turn up in their writings. Their attention dances about, frustrating to teacher or parent but a possible source of creative power. They also like to surprise, perhaps as a way of being themselves in the face of all they're learning. They create incongruities for the fun of it.

• Sound: Rhythm and all the music of talk and poetry, including rhyme, assonance, and alliteration. I also include poems showing repetition, extended lists, and onomatopoeia. A physical cluster of qualities is involved here; there's little barrier between kids and music. Children's great fault, in regard to soundplay, lies in its uncritical use, but they often demonstrate a delicate feel for music in words, especially when the writing is unstructured. Though children need direction, they usually lack the wide command of detail to work well in a highly restrictive form, such as a set rhyme scheme. Their sense of rhythm emerges best when based on their own speech patterns.

• "Moves": By this I mean surprise as a recurrent quality of the language— sophisticated surprise that seems to emphasize the shifts in meaning more than the shock itself.

• Show-don't-tell: Keeping the attention on the sensory, not the abstract.

• Surrealism and metaphor: Images from the mind. Surrealism uses connections from dreams and the unconscious (or connections resembling those); metaphor connects, via one's thought, one object to another, usually in the external world.

• Concision, shapeliness, and understatement: Shortening, shaping, and shutting up.

• Empathy: According to its roots, empathy means "feel in" (whereas sympathy means "feel with"). The quality of reaching outside the self and becoming affected by the circumstances there.

These qualities, which do overlap at any poetic point and are hard to pin down, form the basis of most of my chapter divisions. I wish not to prescribe the reader's understanding but simply to group poems that reverberate in comparable ways for me, with comments, in the hope that clusters of ideas in each case, rather than single dominating ideas, may arise from them.

Chapters 2 thru 5, as well as 16, however, are devoted to particular exercises since some, such as the "I Remember" poem, tend to have qualities somewhat distinct from the others.

In my evaluatory standards I tried to avoid such matters as content, morality, progress in education, conventional logic, skill in mastering given forms—and in fact in these avoidances am going against the grain of normal, beneficial, inevitable teacherly impulse. But this is the "bargain" of creativity. For the sake of verve one allows, even encourages, violations. By so doing, by giving rein to what may include opposition, one hopes to give students the chance for a lively sense of self in what they may write, and hopes that this energy may then come back and vivify the conventional learning, which is of course necessary and much besides, but is also always in danger of fossilizing itself and being merely dead for the schoolchild. The student who has discovered that writing can be lively has an emotional entree not only into literature but into all ways of writing. So I felt emboldened to judge and analyze these works as radically as I could from the (this) artist's point of view.

Many of the poem-by-poem comments are very short; I have not wanted to distract attention from these marvelous pieces with an excess of critical talk, nor to impede their flow. Sometimes I have simply made a brief remark characterizing the piece or its implications. In many cases, however, I've tried to be detailed as well as brief, and in a few cases I've let the poem catalyze a larger thought about poetry.

It is sometimes felt that much of the charm of children's poetry is accidental. I have, however, given the kids credit for whatever I see there, feeling as I do that, while children may not usually be able to intellectualize their poetic moves, the moves they make are derived from the feelings they have, from a natural sense of form or dynamics, and are not purely "accidental." In fact, I find those poetic "hits" that seem unintended by the conscious mind to be more purely poetic.

In the course of the writing portion of a workshop session, I huddle as much as possible with the kids and try to help them with their writing problems (which are often merely "How do you spell 'through?'" but may also involve creative dilemmas). Sometimes I've given them ideas that, sometimes, they've been all too eager to take down verbatim. Unless these are inextricably intertwined with something great the kids have written, I've excluded them.

In most cases, almost routinely, I've corrected spelling. There can be a charm, even an organic charm, to misspellings, but too often they're merely cutesy or heavy-handed in effect. I've corrected grammar, yes and no, case by case, trying to judge each time whether clarity was being violated or an original charm added. I have less often corrected syntax, keeping a spirit of documentary authenticity, respect for the kids' lively lingos. If I thought I surely saw what the kid was trying to "say," and a blunder of haste or ignorance seemed to block or divert it, I've chopped some things away, *very* rarely introduced a word for clarity's sake.

The numbers following the names represent the kids' grade levels in school.

I am grateful to the people who put me in the schools, especially Myra Klahr of the New York State Poets in the Schools program, and to the teachers whose classrooms I visited. I thank Nancy Larson Shapiro for suggesting that I write on this subject, in an article that was seed for this book. I thank Ron Padgett for stepping out of his office one day and asking me to write the book, at a time when that was exactly my heart's private project anyway, and also for being as editor the sort of person one would want to travel with in dangerous country. I thank Alison Dale for a graceful and keen support of what I'm doing. I thank Ted Berrigan, in general and in particular. I thank Kenneth Koch for the smiles I can envision in his classrooms and for being a careful pioneer. And, most of all, thanks to the kids. Keep writing.

INTRODUCTION

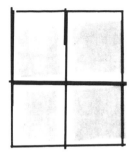

Beyond providing educators with some insights into evoking, evaluating, and encouraging chidren's poetry, this book may give poets and other writers pleasure and food for thought, insights for their own writing. And beyond that, the happy verbal fireworks of these poems could excite anyone who comes within range. But generally speaking, acquaintance with children's poetry is restricted to some poets and some educators. Kenneth Koch's *Wishes, Lies, and Dreams* and other books have spread delight and elucidation in the business, but not much beyond. In some ways children's poems are the least specialized things made of words, but they too tend to fall within the thick-walled cubicles of an age of specialization. The popular media "explosion" blows a diversity of things to the general attention but, unlike real explosions, it's selectively expansive. Poetry, it is feared, might bore the average audience and therefore never reaches it.

One can understand that "high culture" remains off to the side, despite almost universal literacy and the media's proliferation. The audience at large is spoiled by the abundance of immediacy. Anything containing such barriers as complexity, esoteric reference, or the styles of a different era will automatically reduce the audience by the effort required. I propose that there are no significant barriers in or around the poems of children, that the best of them could charm almost anyone, were they only brought to anyone's attention.

As it is, for the kids themselves there's no continuing exposure to poetry in any exciting sense, nor to an atmosphere wherein poetry is considered a vital thing to do, much less a powerful force in society. The term "children's poetry" conjures up a blah sense, in general, of "I love the little flowers,/ They smell so very nice" or some such. That false image is the only barrier, but, unfortunately, an effective one today.

There have been cultures in which poetry has been something current, alive, available to do, for a people in general. I do think it's possible that poetry be as common in people's lives, in *our* society, with a little luck, as say, dancing is, perhaps even more so as people grow older.

A lot of people one meets in America, in every pocket of society, will say that they used to write poetry, when they were kids, and they'll feel either defensive or apologetic about it—not at ease. What they've written usually is descriptions of emotion (young love) or nature philosophy, often rhymed, cast in a fluttery syntax and wooden-legged meter. These are still too often the reductions of poetry commonly available to young people as personal creative models. People outgrow such limits, since their idea of poetry doesn't keep pace with personal development. Poetry has not, as taught, been made real to the individual. Thus it's dropped. (Happily, exceptions grow like grass through old sidewalks.)

But the qualities of poetry are by no means so restricted as that attitude makes them. If one's personal education (in and out of school) holds open a space for such qualities in writing as are shown, for example, in the poems given here, poetic activity will, when it's appropriate, energize that space, and people will sometimes write poems, as they might garden, rollerskate, or sing a song. They may write journals, prose responses and ruminations, letters, stories, experiments, verse—it's all the same in its potential value. And a certain part or angle, of human awareness that is hard to keep alive in the face of life's pressures might be, for many people, kept alive.

●

"Sound is my number" was an early working title for this book. It comes from the final line of this acrostic poem (the first letters of each line form the word "numbers"):

Nothing is more beautiful than a
Universe.
Mama, Mama, give me a
Ball.
East is the way.
Rounding is the sound.
Sound is my number.

The poem was written by a fourth-grade girl, Griselle Gelp, in a school in a part of the South Bronx no one would deny is in many ways devastated. The author is Hispanic and, due to environment, her English language skills are not outstanding, though she's obviously bright.

I once wrote the following short poem:

what I take for drama
thru the windows the brightness
in the blowing snow

is just
natural numbers

and thought well enough of it to include it in a book of my poems, alone on a page. I still like it, as a reminder of a nice attitude. But Griselle's poem clearly outdoes mine. My poem creates perhaps a thoughtful image, "the brightness/ in the blowing snow" to link in one's mind with the fact of the atomic composition of everything. Nevertheless, compared to Griselle's poem, which expresses a similar idea, my lower-case, no-punctuation moves show up as mannerisms. My idea is pushed, stated, too hard grammatically. In her poem the idea arises more naturally, through a dance-like series of gestures that seem inevitable, just right, once they've occurred but that remain surprises. That is, the predictability of mere logic (which is too rigid in my poem) could not in Griselle's poem have led from lines 1 and 2 to lines 3 and 4.

Her first two lines are a beautiful, simple statement, at first blush a huge, Leibniz-like affirmation. The breadth is breath-taking, beyond the scope an adult poet might find "cool." The statement is also deliciously ironic; one "pictures" due to the idea of comparison expressed, a universe laid out, on a table perhaps, with other things so one can examine them and judge the relative beauty. There's also the alternate meaning, that "nothing," that is, a literal absence of things, may be more beautiful than a universe, which is the presence of things. Griselle continues immediately with "Mama, Mama, give me a/ Ball." Meaning-wise, this has to be an appeal to the creative powers for Earth to live on; intellectually it fits the previous statement perfectly, but what a jump it is! The tone of the language is over at the other end of the spectrum. Then, with impeccable brevity and a good ear, she brings the sense of the poem down through direction ("East," perhaps for sunrise or mysticism) and planet-shape ("Rounding") to the last statement, "Sound is my number," which seems to say she finds exactitude, measure, in the music of the world about her. The change from "the" to "my" helps this focusing-in process. The fact that the last line uses the singular "number" in an acrostic whose spine word is the plural ("numbers") seems to show us, modestly, that this is one "number" among many possible numbers.

Compared with all this, which seems sheer inspiration to me, my poem appears calculated. The way the last four words are set off and the line-break after "just" (to let trickle out the other meaning of "just"), are too portentous. It feels like a false concision, whereas her remarks have natural economy. Her words have the air that "primitive" art has, at best, an absence of self-image or intentionality, just a natural expression like a wild animal or waterfall.

We can learn matters of great value from works like this — all manner of returns to the basic, unsullied poetic shot-in-the-dark. However, there are many turns of phrase, image, and thought that we could not "get away with" in our own work, simply because they would seem false to the relative sophistication anyone must assume is part of our mental makeup as educated adults. The only way to get around this would be to build up a life's body of work as a naif, to, in other words, validate for oneself, over a period of time, a childlike stance toward reality. In a way, poets have always done this, but there is a certain license, knowing these poems are by children, that is a part of our appreciation of them. We grant them the innocence from which their words can shine. It is hard for adults, when we write, to keep from qualifying the quick lights that may appear (do I put "come to us" instead of "appear" for the alliteration?) (no, "too much").

If an adult wrote the following lune (three words/five words/three words is the rule)

> My dog bites
> and I answer the door.
> I am happy.

how would it be perceived, in the poetry world now? It would depend heavily on context. Do individual poems always depend on context? Do short poems? Does a typical fragility in children's poetry show up in a need for context—that is, are their successes often in the cloudy realm of ambiguity? If so, is this poetic or unsubstantial? How *should* this small poem be perceived?

One response I've received to this lune is that "bites" is a mistake for "barks." If this is the case, the poem takes on a different power from the one that I, in my literalness, get. "Barks" gives it the charm of extreme plainness; natural simplicity leaves room for the opening of the door to stand out. As the piece is, with "bites," the effect is more surrealistic; the opening stands out by means of surprise juxtaposition. In either case, the simplicity of utterance acts as a transparency to the vision, doesn't get in the way. The vision concentrates itself in the opening of the door ("answer" is the word, as if the door had spoken; simplicity helps us notice the oddities of our own idiom). To me, there's something about the "I am happy" that goes beyond any expectable joy. I think of a passage in Jack London's *White Fang*, read in childhood, in which a wolf cub comes for the first time out to the cave entrance and its world is suddenly expanded via the sight in a very heady way, through ridge after ridge, rocks and blue haze, to a representation of the fears and potentialities the larger world may be for us. I'm not at all saying that this poem refers to this passage, even unconsciously, merely that there's a touch of unspecified magic in the way the opening of the door is left a bit mysterious. Our attention is drawn to "opening" in a general way.

At this point I should speak of "reading into" kids' poems what may not be intended. Yes, of course I do this. I believe all poetry is, in part, a field for reading-into. The process of poetry is not just the conveyance to the reader of an intended thought; if it were, an essay would be more direct. We think of words as being merely pragmatic sound-units, invented to carry denotative information. "Pass the salt." "Mr. Peabody has only two fingers on his left hand." But language is organic; as it grows, psychological expressivity and practicality are intertwined. Not only do we utilize tones and connotations, rhythm, and other musical effects, to make our points with speech, we also *reveal* ourselves constantly in many complex ways, even when we try not to. Poetry capitalizes on these qualities of revelation. At best, mastery and subconscious revelation work, almost paradoxically, together to mingle the known and the unknown. All this, of course, does not absolve one from "reading-into" excesses. But it may give us a basis for respecting the validity of a poem's *expansiveness*.

The revelatory qualities of poetry stand out more conspicuously in children's poetry, by and large, than in the poems of adults. The conscious mind stands less in the way. This is both a glory and a frailty. Of course Gri-

selle Gelp did not have the metaphysics of her "Sound is my number" poem intellectualized and articulated. In a way, it was perhaps a lucky hit, that is, she
might not be able to write a body of poetry consistent with that startling vision.
But who would? Even an adult's education, which does inculcate a certain consistency, leaves artists at the eventual mercy of inspired occasions for their really
memorable works. Kids, without the glue of education, even more so.

I do believe that the connections I see in Griselle's poem are valid, that she had
a series of feelings that were triggered by choosing the word "numbers" for an
acrostic poem, and that once she'd had the inspiration of starting with "nothing"
and then coming up with "universe" she was involved in a happy conflict that
didn't become too mentally "set" for her. Such is the fine flexibility of youth. In
the magic moments, good words do pop up for us, out of the blue. We can't explain them, perhaps, but they refer to something genuine inside us. We all know
such moments, even in an everyday sense, in talk or thought. The unbidden
nature of insight formed in words is familiar, not esoteric.

I use as example the poem about the dog, the door, and the happiness partly
because it's not clearly great. Its effect is ambiguous, not necessarily a fault,
nor a virtue. But when a kid makes such a move as that in a poem, we know it
is not a sophistry; we give credit at least to the authenticity of the impulse
(which, by itself, carries us a long way into possibilities of poetry).

The feeling that the impulse is authentic to the author, not derivative, carries a lot of the excitement of poetry for me. This is especially true among very
young poets, in whose works one could not reasonably expect the more "solid"
qualities of good writing. But beyond this understanding, I admit to a bias for
the "primitive" aspects of poetry. This is not definable by such trappings as
vocabulary, or anything at all referentially recognizable — I'm not speaking of
the *subject* of the poem but the mode of language. It's matter of riskiness, or
rather obliviousness of risk, in the face of pressures to be civilized.

Children have a built-in context of innocence — not that we don't know they
can be tricky as any devil, but their language in many ways is close to, and
readily reflects, the primal impulses of language (rhythm, perception, thing,
"idea," desire). How to keep that touch alive and still grow up able and mature
in the given world, how to be responsible *and* responsive, is the problem they
will face and feel but may never notice.

As to teaching the child, where do we go from there? I can only suggest
study and discipline that still allows sensitivity to the serendipitous. Anyone
who starts at poetry very young is liable to undergo a "sophomore jinx" of
some kind, wherein beginner's luck, which is an ecstasy of sorts, wears off and
the replacement by solidity of approach just isn't as vivid. Those children who
do maintain an interest in creative writing will have to solve a lot of problems
by themselves. The teacher can encourage, judiciously moderate and make a
lot of good things available, e.g., books but not only books, since such things as
paintings, animals, and wooden spoons also inspire a poet — not only by what
they are (their content) but also formally, by how they look, feel, sound, grow,
and move.

The teacher can also help nurture the creative spirit in children by finding her or his way to different standards — in evoking, handling, judging kids' poetry—than those applied to most other areas in education. Many have done so. I hope that this book may contribute to an understanding of what such standards might be, and of how there may be precise evaluations that do not really fall under the term "standards" — less codifiable values but values nonetheless, full of both suggestiveness and accuracy. The main fallacy in judging poetry has been that these two qualities are not seen as partners.

Chapter I

HOW I TEACH POETRY IN THE SCHOOLS

The focal point of the school, organizational-ly and mood-wise, is the principal. School principals, I find, may be helpful or not par-ticularly, or may delegate helpfulness, but seldom trouble the poetry program as long as one is on time and seems confident. There's little, however, the visiting poet can do about the mood of the whole school. One operates class by class, where the teachers are supremely important. The teacher is the bellwether of the class, of its developed attention. When the teacher writes along with the students, or simply listens alertly, this participa-tion catalyzes the whole room.

On a more practical note, the teacher can exert authority, which the visiting poet doesn't have, when it's needed for the proper degree of order. For me, qui-etness is important when poems are being read aloud, and it's an eternal little battle to bring classes "down" after the hurly-burly of creation. Essentials are learned in each state, the listening state and the composing state, that can't be fully absorbed in the other. When the students are writing, however, it's amazing how a fair to great degree of noisiness, when it's mostly about the mat-ter at hand, can not only fail to dim the concentration but actually enhance it, act as a matrix of energy.

My first visit I jump right into things by telling the kids what we're going to do: talk about poems (not much) and read poems aloud (adults', children's), all building up to the main thing—having them write (using a different basic idea each class session, explained, with plenty of examples). Then I'll collect pieces, read them aloud (*anonymously*) with top-of-the-head comments, take home and type *some* ("Don't feel bad if yours isn't chosen—one or more'll probably show up along the way"), hand out copies next time I come if the rexo machines are working, and put together an anthology at the end. Any questions? At this point I read two poems aloud, often using "Too Blue" by Lang-ston Hughes and "Crossing" by Philip Booth (see Appendix), discuss them briefly in down-to-earth ways, which these works by their nature encourage. Then, as first exercise, I prescribe I Remember poems, reading aloud one of mine first, then a bunch from kids, and emphasizing detail ("Don't just write 'I remember going to the movies with my friend Yvonne,' period, end of memory; tell whatever there was about it that made it stick in your mind; make a pic-ture of the scene out of words"). The students write for fourteen minutes or so; I walk around, answering questions, talking or not talking as seems appro-priate. Then I collect the papers and read them aloud, praising the "hits" I perceive in each poem, timing this feedback for the last ten minutes of class. Then out. Next free period I mark the ones I'm going to type. Later at home I type them up, which honors the kids, makes palpable what they've done, and preserves it. Then bring 'em back alive.

In subsequent sessions I try to keep a balance going between content-orient-ed exercises (writing about places, for example) and devices, such as acrostics and lunes, that tend to give the students a technical lead from line to line and to leave content free. With the exception of I Remember's, Chants, Animal Poems, and Collaborations—covered as units in the next four chapters—and a miscellaneous batch of exercises lumped into Chapter 16, the following are the chief writing exercises from which the poems and pieces in this book arose.

ACROSTIC POEMS

The acrostic is an admirable form for student use. There's only one letter of requirement per line, which gives enough to go on (kids are often at sea without something leading on) but doesn't over-dictate. The form's lightness tends to stimulate surreal juxtapositions and other originalities. Also, the re-quirement comes at the line beginning (not at the end, as with rhyme), so once the letter is worded the rhythm is free. Acrostics encourage interesting line-breaks, show the kids that lines are not just sentences, or thoughts, but also sound units and fragmentation devices. The form abets the development of subtle, surprising, "off" connections between spine word and text, as well as the economy of lists and near-lists (elimination of connectives). In presenting the acrostic, I tell the students something like the following.

Write a word vertically, down the paper, and use its letters to begin the lines of a poem that you then make up. The poem should have *something* to do with the spine word, but it can be some weird or hard-to-see connection; don't make it just an explanation of the word. You don't have to rhyme. Lines can be as long or short as you like, and you can break your lines right in the middle of a thought or phrase. This sometimes makes the words stand out in a new and in-teresting way, like cracking open a rock and finding a little blue cave in it. Skip a line going down for each letter of your spine word in case you come up with a long poem-line that won't fit on one line of paper. Use your imaginations; don't be afraid to sound crazy; it often means you've come up with new ideas; try things out.

I show them a good acrostic (by a student) on the board, then write the spine words for about twelve or fifteen more and read off the poems, pointing to the beginning letters as I go. Naturally I choose an assortment that will display a big range of acrostic possibilities.

PLACE POEMS

Sometimes I begin by showing the students "Nantucket" by William Carlos Williams (see Appendix), and point out how all the physical things mentioned add up to a light-colored, quiet mood. I say that one way to express the feeling of a place is to pick out one thing or one little view, one part of the place, express it, and let it stand for the whole.

I talk up places, how we have such strong feelings for them early on (even Mother's cradling arm is a "place" to a new baby) and ask them to write about a place they know well, could be their room, the block they walk and play on every day, etc., or a place they've seen once or rarely but that made a vivid impression. I read them a bunch of kids' pieces on place, drawing attention to the epiphanies, good parts, accumulations. I urge them to write with the effort of recalling detail, maybe close their eyes and picture the place first. Think of it as a one-minute travelogue in words, don't leave out anything that may help recreate the live scene. I ask for "poems" (line-breaks, metaphors, possible swift changes of image, going by feel); often the pieces come out prose anyway, which can also be fine.

LUNES

The lune is a simplification of formal haiku. Instead of counting syllables in the three lines, which might make kids overly concerned with the mere mechanics, one counts words: three/five/three, any subject, any mood. With lots of good examples given and discussed, the students do abundantly demonstrate a fine apprehension of the power of tiny, non-expositional, word-by-word effects, plus the necessity of balanced rhythm, which looms large in a short piece. Thus there's a push toward the knowledge that ideas do not exist without their expressive articulations, and the importance of language "per se" is brought home.

> When the sun's
> rays hit the shades, it
> lights up lines.

This piece (dashed off by a Nebraska 5th grader years ago) excellently illustrates the possibility of poetry being plain talk of the immediate environment (sun striking venetian blinds on classroom window). It is also a deceptively complex maze of sound correspondences and play: simple rhythms in lines one and three contrasting with syncopation of line two (differing syllable lengths, comma pause, consonantal percussion), n's around soft "the" in line 1 forming a sound-swing, "rays-shades" assonance and "hit-it" rhyme, soft central "the" repeated, five terminal s's, 'lights-lines," "sun's-up," n again in "lines," t in "lights"—until "lights up lines" carries more import that the physical window pattern alone. The lines of the poem are lit up too. I advise students that the author probably didn't calculate all this but that a careful, though nonspecific, concentration can let the musical phrases come.

Surprise in the short, third line (especially) is a common vivifier of lunes. A change of "voice" and/or rhythm can help the change of meaning snap to, or *be* the change in meaning.

> Go to Heaven.
> If it's nice, call me.
> I'll be there.

Rhyme can sometimes work well in lunes, but it's like loading a heavy rock into a small boat. I tell them lunes are like Crackerjacks, the more you..., etc. That I once wrote 100 in an evening and by the end everything I saw or thought registered in my brain three/five/three, and that I told a junior high class this and a girl came back the next day with 120, all solid little word-pieces from what was around her, especially at home. Sometimes I tell them lunes are like looking through a crack; even the plainest sight may look interesting, due to the focus.

Again, reading aloud many good examples by kids—with admonitions not to copy their wordings or ideas—helps the students see their own possibilities. It is amazing what variety may evolve and what compression is possible in these eleven-word poems.

WILLIAM CARLOS WILLIAMS IMITATIONS

On the black board I show the kids the following two poems by Dr. Williams.

THIS IS JUST TO SAY   ●

I have eaten
the plums
that were in
the icebox

and which
you were probably
saving for breakfast

Forgive me
they were delicious
so sweet
and cold

so much depends
upon

a red wheel
barrow

glazed with rain
water

beside the white
chickens

4

I ask them first to write a poem apologizing for something "bad" they have done, imaginary or real. I point out how the *s* sounds in the last three lines of the first poem help bring out the mouth-watering goodness of the plums, making the poem a sorry-not-sorry balancing act. I urge them not to "copy" too closely.

Then I discuss the second poem, how it gently spotlights neglected things of everyday life, and ask them to write a similar piece out of their own experience, like a snapshot in words.

In both cases I read them a variety of children's poems along these lines. The "apologies" tend to be funny, and the "wheelbarrow" pieces tend to be delicate. The kids usually divide things into short lines without prompting (or I'll tell them it helps display the rhythms of speech). Both exercises can be done in a single class period.

THING POEMS

I talk up the wonders of common but relatively unnoticed objects — hand, egg, floor, sky, hair, river, piece of bread — and ask them to write in prose or poetry about one of them. I urge them to get beyond the expectable sentiments that gather about familiar things ("Don't write, 'The beautiful egg contains growing life'"). Sometimes I read them Gary Snyder's "Hay for the Horses" or Denise Levertov's "Pleasures" (see Appendix)—and always some examples by kids — to build up a thingy mood.

"REAL-LIFE" WRITINGS

I ask the students to think of some event, big or small ("It could be about a floating speck of dust"), that they saw, did, or had happen to them lately enough that they remember a lot of details, and to write about it. I try for something more like a snapshot than a narrative, in the sense that it's a moment with many details of the scene visible. I advise them to recreate a little world/instant in words and, when they have made it real and solid, to, as it were, float it off via simile or metaphor, throw out line or lines to the rest of reality. Something like "When the blue car bumped into the brown bakery truck on 181st St., the car doors flew open like the wings of a gull trying to take off from the harbor waters." As always, I read them plenty of examples first and, in this case, I make up spontaneously an example of "painting a scene" (rather than just mentioning the salient action), with use of specific terms, colors, names, weather, corner-of-the-eye stuff, etc.

The results often violate my prescription but work anyway, when empathy has been activated.

ABOUT POETRY

Reserved for the last day. I ask them to write about poetry or about the process of writing, not in general terms ("poetry is nice," "poetry is boring"), but something palpable, something that moves, or to make a little myth of it, experiment, show not tell, find wild thoughts somehow felt even if the mind can't explain the connection, try anything out. I invite them to include negative thoughts, difficulties; poetry is not peaches and cream, can be frustrating, tiresome, disturbing, whatever. The pieces can be in a variety of forms. This "exercise" has resulted in a great number of the most amazing catches, thoughts, and images I've seen.

> Poetry is a
> slow flash
> of light
> because it comes
> to you piece by
> piece.

●

I think of my general approach as organic, inductive, building from the children's familiars up, rather than teaching them intricate forms to master, or attempting to initiate them into a sophisticated sensibility. Time enough for that, and to avoid its pitfalls, when and if they have written personally for some while, and of course writing personally in some strong sense is what the most developed poetry still is. Heavy programming from me at this point would draw out less of their particular gifts.

This part of the school curriculum is different from most of the rest, in that it is more a matter of learning from the inside out. On the other hand, ask a kid to write something expressing his soul and he'll be lost. People this young need a guide, albeit a light guide. So I use devices, even gimmicks, which tend to balance between requesting and allowing poems, between spontaneity and concentration, until the two merge.

I try to get things across to the students by example, not by concept. On the other hand, the simple exhortation "be original" can slam things open. I tell them papers can be messy, this is a workshop, no time to rewrite for beauty's sake, scratchouts show you're thinking. We'll make 'em pretty later. I also find that down-to-earth explanations, in detail, of sound nuances and, within the kids' experience, other fine points as well go over readily with them. Matters such as the vowel progressions in the "Red Wheelbarrow" piece, or say, the connotative values in Denise Levertov's poem of things found on the beach (see Appendix).

Being in a class is a peculiar combination, for me, of formal and informal. Given the formal situation of standing in the front of a classroom with a specific, quasi-teacher role, I "try" to be quite informal and natural (and still get things done fast). I always stand or walk around rather than sit. I toss bits of chalk, stutter, scratch, cross my feet, glance out the window, talk as I would talk to a trusted friend (but limiting vocabulary and referential scope), never smile unless it pops up, use humor freely, don't pretend to be hip but let my colloquial self come out, don't praise falsely (they "know"), try to be aware of the room energy. Each workshop leader will find his or her most workable way of being there.

In this very human, though structured, situation known as the classroom, energy counts for more than ideas. And the energy must be transferable. It can be low-key as long as it's felt. Speechifying about one's passions for and even concepts of poetry is self-indulgence. Isolated opinions vaporize, the loftier the quicker. One is a communicator in this situation, not pushing things and convictions into the students' faces but getting workable ideas within reach, or into the fuzzy area just outside normal reach, which is also "reach," in the right light.

In longer residencies and/or with older kids I may ask for out-of-class poems. Especially when the assignment's left open, they usually turn out poorly. The kids, with leisure and without the hot hullaballoo of the classroom common endeavor, tend to revert to sentimental cloudiness specific only in being derivative. Post-puberty is a time of overblown soul (and its flip side, cynicism). Here, however, with older kids, revision may enter (in my "Pied Piper" residency experience, elementary school kids have little patience or perspective for extensive revision). Gently, one can ask for particulars. Gently, one can focus on rhythm and sound, consistency of thought (if appropriate), even on originality of expression.

The purpose of having a poet in a given class is not to produce thirty full-blown lifelong poets but to touch the kids with poetry, with a feeling for art that may grow from specifics outward for many years and affect many of their responses to daily things, that their lives may be open a touch more to inner and outer vividness. I ask them at the end simply to keep writing—journals, poems, anything. I ask them to do it sometimes, when they can, when they feel like it, for the rest of their lives, as they might, sometimes, dance.

No one person includes all viewpoints. That is, we each have taste. My taste is in part only personal, and I'm sure this affects the way the kids I visit write. And how I *like* what they write. This is true of every writing teacher. The solution is not to devitalize one's presentation in a vain urge for perfect objectivity but simply to examine rigorously one's preferences in poetry and, if they still seem worthy, to act on them without apology (and still close no doors).

Chapter II

I REMEMBER

"I remember when I smelled a rose the whole thing broke"

The first day's writing in my workshops is usually in the form of "I Remember" poems (invented by Joe Brainard). Each line of the poem (and a line can be of *any* length) begins with the words "I remember." The students are encouraged to use details in the relating of personal memories, in the terms and music of ordinary talk. The matter of details needs a lot of pushing, since kids, though having the fresh eye, often lack faith in the importance of the personal fact. They are beginning to use generalization to order their world and will produce unedifying essences like "I remember my first day in school" (end of memory). Lively examples are best for urging detail. The songlike repetition of "I remember" tends to isolate the bits of content, to engender a sharp focus that brings out the energy of the daily-life material.

> I remember when the triplets were born. We all went in a hospital and we were in a waiting room, and boy was I nervous. I couldn't keep still. I had so much to eat I felt like my stomach weighed a ton. The father-to-be (my uncle that is) was very shaky. A lot of stupid thoughts were going through my head like what am I going to wear the next day and did I miss anything on TV? And all of a sudden this little short man came in and asked, was this the Reid family and, believe it or not, there was over 20 of us and everyone answered yes and he said to the father-to-be, you have a son, and all the guys was really overjoyed, and then the doctor said, a girl, and all us girls were jumping up and down acting crazy, and he said another boy baby was born. I never felt so good in my life. I was a Godmother of three...
> —Lisa M. Reid, 8th

The excited, brass-tacks tone is just right for evoking a feeling of immediacy. The piece is like captured talk. "Boy was I nervous," "weighed a ton," "little short man," and "acting crazy" are all expressively accurate, in part *because* they are factually inaccurate or grammatically wrong. Vernacular prose. The frankness of the "stupid thoughts" sentence refreshes the whole piece. The very long sentence beginning "all of a sudden" gives the sense of the rush of events. The whole things flows like warm water, happily continuous with "and's."

> I remember my first pair of black shoes.
> I remember putting on my mother's clothing.
> I remember falling for the third time.
> I remember trying to fly from my rocking chair.
> I remember asking my cat to dance with me.
> I remember my grandfather and I swimming in the beach, with
> the roaring waves.
> I remember when my grandmother and I had our first fight
> and I tried to throw her out the window.
> I remember the eighth time I punched my friend Doris on the
> nose.
> I remember so many things that I sometimes don't remember.
> —Odalya Camero, 7th

A more typical "I remember" series. The rapid juxtaposition of scattered daily-life items add up to a sense of reality, with its facts and its unpredictable progress. In this case the verbs are especially action-packed. The sequence of putting on/falling/fly/dance/swimming/roaring/throw out/punched makes a graph of movement in the reader's mind, enlivening the whole as music does a song's lyrics. That the first and last items are the only static ones makes the in-between turmoil swell and fade like a parabola.

> I remember when I was one I started to walk to the door.
> I remember I was lying in the sand looking up in the sky see-
> ing seagulls flying.
> I remember picking flowers when all of a sudden a bee stung
> me right on the leg.
> I remember arguing with my sister about her doll just because
> I broke it.
> —Melissa Rosa, 3rd

The items seem randomly ordered but may be seen as a series — enterprise/meditation/pain/battle—representing chief divisions of life. Free association is a part of the "I remember" device — in provocative contrast to the typical daily-surface emphasis of the content within each item—and often has its own inner logic. That is, it's not for nothing that one thinks of one thing after another, even if they seem unconnected.

> I remember when I threw my brother a cup of soda at his face.
> I remember playing with my cousin's dancing-playing-hearing
> record, turning the lights off, playing the drums, acting like a
> ghost.
> I remember taking water and then spitting all over the house.

> I remember putting ketchup in a water gun and saying to my
> brother, "I killed you, I am very foolish." What a happy time
> we had.
> —*Evelyn Cardenas, 5th*

Catastrophe looms large in memory, and is more easily spoken of than its opposite. Children's "I Remember" poems are frequently litanies of disaster. This one has the relative harmlessness of being mostly liquid mischief plus the charms of "acting like a ghost" and "I killed you, I am very foolish," which by their oddity jar us into a keener attention, illumine more particularly the person talking and being shown.

> I remember the day my hands got stuck under my window sill
> and I cried so hard I farted.
> —*Anonymous, 4th*

The candidness required is quite touching. Simplicity of utterance carries no trace of qualification or justification, nor of "disarming" frankness, as would be almost unavoidable in an adult. Just the facts. Purity, in a fart.

> I remember on my first birthday when everyone was singing
> Happy Birthday to me, I didn't understand because I was only a
> little girl that had just turned one year old.
> —*Priscilla Wherry, 5th*

Simple grace of statement. An adult would have a hard time transcending embarrassment at the truism (I was too young to understand), thus be ironic and lose it.

> I remember my first watch. I opened it to take out the Mickey
> Mouse.
> —*Veronica Fernandez, 5th*

The logic of being interested in something, for a child, doesn't stop short of touch. Adults are often content with distance. This "I Remember" item shows that insight via pure fact. And "take out the Mickey Mouse" has an odd, concise charm. But, despite the directness, the delight is in an *implication*, the destruction of the watch. It's this dynamic—that the hearer draws his own conclusion, the sense that he has *participated* in an insight — that draws laughter whenever this is read aloud. If it were more explanatory ("I wrecked it by opening it") the effect would not be there.

> I remember eating sand when there wasn't anything else to do.
> I remember reading my first book in fifth grade, and reading it
> eight times in a row because it was good.
> —*Claudia Bravo, 8th*

Extremes shown as natural. Why not eat sand? Interesting texture. Why not do a good thing over and over?

> I remember when a car almost hit me I turned green.
> —*Jorge Manguel, 7th*

Sudden visual exaggeration from a real base, like a picture, say, of a cartoon caveman opening the door of a photographed living room. The play of the real "almost" happening and the exaggerated, the turning green, actually (in the "story") doing so, extends the sense of reality, refreshing to our overly scientific powers of belief.

> I remember when a bike ran over me and it felt good 'cause I just felt the wheels and I wanted him to run over me again.
> —Belkis Feliz, 6th

Ability to observe with the senses even when it runs contrary to convention. The convention is that to be run over is painful, but "just felt the wheels" shows us there wasn't a crash, bump, or tear, just an instant of massage.

> I remember when I first came here I didn't know English. My grandfather had told me that in the United States gum was growing on trees and eggs also. Since I was very young when I got here I was checking out the trees. I remember I became real sad when I saw the trees without leaves and this wind that blew my hat away. The worst part was when I got to school. They had placed me in an English class and the teacher didn't understand me and I didn't understand her. I would cry in school until I met Ana Ventura, my first friend over here. She knew a little bit of English so we hung around together. By the time I got to first grade I could understand and speak English a little. Today my English is better than my Spanish.
> —Amy Almonte, 8th

The story is touching because it is unaffected. Such perky details as "gum" (instead of gold), and "checking out the trees," and the lovely change to a disposition of winter (trees/no leaves/wind blew/hat/"away") take it away from the sense of being merely "an old story." Even such a small, unemphasized touch of syntax as "over here" brings out emotion by understatement, so much seems compressed in the word "over."

> I remember when I was sitting on a tree and a dog kissed me.
> I remember when I went to the movies and all I did was close my eyes.
> —Mayra, 3rd

The poignancy of childhood passivity, told in two ways.

> I remember when I smelled a rose the whole thing broke.
> I remember my birthday. One person came.
> —Ana Torres, 3rd

The same as above, with a rueful tinge of humor in the language centered in "the whole thing," in the word "broke," and in the shortness of the sentences in the second line.

> I remember when I was little in kindergarten I met my friend

> Gia. When we had snack I brought crackers and she brought
> grapes, and we put it together and ate it.
> —*Renee Breazzano, 5th*

The natural sense of *pace*, especially in the second sentence, lets the purity of
the incident relax in the rhythm.

> I remember when I was five years old and I had a bear big as me.
> I remember when my grandfather died when I was six and they
> picked me up to see him.
> —*Lattice Williams, 6th*

In each case, the geometry actualizes the space. We feel immediacy because
size or movement has made it pictorial. Thus emotion has a base to rise from.

> I remember when I flopped down in a chair and closed my eyes.
> —*Maria La Rocca, 6th*

Beautifully small. Recognizable emotionally via minimal fact.

> I remember when my sister was in the shower and she was sing-
> ing and she was singing "*Oh my darling*" and then I snuck in the
> bathroom without her even hearing and then I flushed the toilet
> and hot water went on and she got burnt.
> —*Joey DiGarbo, 2nd*

That the song is "Oh my darling" makes for wild contrast, Chaplinesque
humor. The repetition of "and she was singing" brings out vernacular music.

> I remember when my sister and I had the first fight. We didn't talk
> to each other for days. She kept slipping notes under the door, but I
> didn't know how to read so I just kept giving them back.
> —*Ida Caputo, 4th*

The type of so-avoidable misunderstanding often exploited in the movies for
an agonizing audience involvement ("*Tell* her!").

> I remember a beautiful raven fighting with an old brown
> woodpecker.
> —*Kristina Lacognata, 4th*

"Beautiful" and "old brown" combine surprise and opposition without reducing either. That is, given "beautiful," "old brown" is more of a change than an
opposite would be.

> I remember when I said to my mommy and daddy "I love you." It
> was just this morning.
> —*Melissa Kawecky, 3rd*

Time jumps suddenly but gently in the second sentence's revelation.

> I remember when I was in the Dominican Republic swimming
> in the ocean, dancing to the Spanish music, going to sleep
> under a tree.

> I remember eating the fresh fruits from the trees, picking up
> apples, oranges and coffee.
> —*Yanick Pena, 8th*

In the two lines, action is grounded to sleep and fruit to coffee.

> I remember seeing a comb outside on the street a long time ago. It
> was green.
> —*Sandra Martinez, 5th*

Such a small fact remembered refreshes our appreciation of little things. It also draws our attention to memory itself rather than to the content of the memory. Poems often seem unworkable when the subject is too commanding; a slight subject allows nuances to stir about. The brevity of the second sentence here makes the vivid sense of "green" overlap the contemplative distance of "a long time ago," and the senses conflict interestingly, like wet paint on a thought.

> I remember trying to lose weight because my cousin was com-
> ing and she thinks she's a bigshot, and when she came she
> was as fat as the fat lady in the circus.
> I remember I was in a play and when I got on stage I wasn't in
> the play at all.
> I remember talking to my friend about myself, and when I
> finished she wasn't there.
> —*Danielle Stone, 6th*

Item 1, the moves of a short story. Item 2, a hall of mirrors effect. Item 3, a combination of both elements. The way the three work together, with people scattering from one's thoughts of them in various ways, shows a complex personality.

> I remember when I was in third grade and my best friend liked
> the same guy until we found out he was making love letters to
> Nancy Grand. I remember when my best friend and I gave the
> biggest Halloween party ever and he left Nancy so he could get
> some soda. My friend was dressed as a man so she asked Nancy for
> a dance. Nancy was so romanced dancing she did not know she
> was on the edge of the swimming pool. As she fell she cried out,
> saying, "Oh you rude gentle man!"
> —*Eyerilis Fernandez, 5th*

The oddity of "making" love letters forces a fresh look at the word and at what is done to produce a love letter. "Making" love letters seems a solider venture than "sending" or even "writing" them, thus a greater challenge to the frustrated girl duo. The speed and economy of statement make the introduction of the third girl, Nancy, coming right after the second girl, a socko expansion. "Biggest...ever" by its exaggeration casts the event into the archetype-familiarity of myth or fairy-tale. "Romanced dancing" is both odd and concise and adds the musical focus of rhyme. "As she fell" skips over the push, but we know it more quickly than if we had been told. There is a formal, poker-faced tone (effective by contrast with the content), in "As she fell she cried out, saying." The phrase "Oh you rude gentle man!" charms by its oddness, intensifies the slight fairy-tale flavor, illuminates the paradox in the "man's" both dancing and dousing.

> I remember going to the store with my uncle and I got shot.
> I remember going to the school and they mugged me.
> I remember going to the movies and a monster tried to eat me.
> I remember going home and my mother was not there.
> I remember going to my friend's house and he would not let
>   me play.
> I remember going to the park with my friends and one of them
>   hit me in the head with a ball.
> I remember making new friends and one of them hit me with a
>   spitball.
> I remember watching TV and it broke on me because I kicked it.
>   —Danny Santiago, 5th

Again memory coughs up catastrophe, which is more believable and interesting than blessedness, leaves one less vulnerable when expressed. There's a shift of reality level from "shot" and "mugged" to the monster line, and that shift retroactively changes the light in which we take the first two lines, introduces playfulness. Also, the abruptness, lack of transitional devices, lets the change simply be there, in a quasi-physical way. Adults often lose poetry via attempts at palatability of shift. The understatement, then, of "mother was not home," the lack of ornament, shows that mere absence can be as disastrous as violent attacks are. Then the piece goes off into a humorous accumulation of futility, with a mea culpa bow at the end. A shapely, funny (but not whimsical) confession.

> I remember when there was a fire in my building. I went to
> school. Everyone asked me what happened. I was so happy.
>   —Gilma Alvarez, 5th

An adult would not, generally, admit so clearly that the happiness of getting attention could supplant the fear proper to a building fire. And simplicity makes it stand out.

> I remember the day I had to go away down to the lake.
> I remember the water was light like the sunlight. In the early
>   morning.
>   —Oyelino Genao, 5th

"In the early morning." If this sentence fragment were written by an adult, I would think it a derivative attempt at poetic tone. But because I trust a kid, this kid, not to have mixed that much in literary style, I'm brought back to the thing expressed, a key slant on the identity of water and light, in lake dawn. I am stuck with having a positive response to ignorance, but the "ignorance" is a transparency for pure observation.

> I remember when it was snowing, all of that snow comes from
> the blue sky and ends up on the street.
> —*Cynthia Gomez, 6th*

The child's touch, syntactically, is the use of the term "blue sky" (not just "sky"). The presence of "blue" makes the color (white) of the snow implicit, which in turn brings out the complicated color and all of the street. All because "blue" was mentioned.

> I remember when I locked myself in the bathroom in the dark.
> The darkness came over me like a monster and swept my feet
> with fear.
> —*David Kalicharan, 6th*

"Swept my feet." A perfect kid's-observation. That the feet were chosen makes the monstrousness more inclusive (head to foot), but the verb "swept" is the crux. It's used without "through" or "over," the cliche accompaniments of "swept," and therefore we get a dizzying sense of motion.

> I remember when a car hit me and I jumped up into the hot air.
> —*James Guasp, 6th*

"Hot" makes the car real. With the presence of temperature, the car is no longer merely a hitting thing. The air heat, being sensory, reminds us of the car's heat, motor, smells, dirt, metal, gas.

> I remember the day I was taking piano lessons, my fingers stopped
> all of a sudden.
> —*Georgina Fernandez, 6th*

How the bare recitation of fact may release emotion more fully than any push. The sensitivity of the reader is tickled out here, by understatement, to an em-pathetic understanding.

> I remember at night, when the white dots smiled at me. I couldn't
> sleep, I couldn't eat. I just remember they smiled at me.
> —*Tommy Kim, 5th*

Here we jump to a rendition of things that is affected by dream, or the bits and tinges of dream that enter waking life. Trying to picture a dot smiling takes us beyond normal dimension. "I couldn't eat" is, first, natural-seeming because it's a prefabricated usage, then funny, because the kid's presumably in bed in the middle of the night and what would he be doing eating? The last line makes it poignant.

> I remember when I first saw my grandma and she was so fat I
> almost fainted, but I just let that go.
> —*Anonymous, 5th*

The exaggeration of "fainted" suddenly turned by swift, cool run of real talkflow "but I just let that go." Non-explanatory, thus rhythmically true to the moment, since the explanatory mode, being cerebral, tends to lose touch with rhythm.

> I remember when I learned how to jump, I was so happy that I jumped.
> —*Rosita Vasquez, 4th*

A natural joke.

> I remember when I was born. It was the happiest day of my life.
> —*Lenore Garcia, 4th*

Irony but altogether unforced by connotative word values, as adult irony usually is.

> I remember the day I bought a rabbit and it died right in my face.
> —*David Fergus, 4th*

"Right in my face": a beautiful way of emphasizing the strength and in-evitability of connections; as if dying were expansive physically as it is psychically.

> I remember first getting a fever and feeling like someone was ironing me.
> —*Nicholas Tanery, 6th*

An excellent metaphor, simply because it's original, obviously from the experi-ence and not from literary reference. A common mistake in teaching metaphor is to concentrate on the mechanics of it. This works better in, for example, alliteration, where the object is music, not idea. But the whole poetic point as far as idea goes is originality of vision. There's no advantage in teaching thirty more children to say that clouds are like puffs of cotton.

> I remember when I was a baby that I opened one eye.
> —*Jenny Sanchez, 4th*

and

> I remember when I was born I didn't even know myself.
> —*Alfredo Placencia, 4th*

Reality meets fantasy, minimally put.

> I remember when my bird was singing.
> I remember when my dog was dancing.
> I remember when I was touching the sun.
> I remember when I got a new snake.
> I remember the time I saw God.
> —*Fran, 1st*

A graph of degrees of real and fantastic in seamless terms. That is, even the jump to God, by that time, seems like just another part of her thought.

The next sixteen selections combine everyday reality and fantasy, a matrix of fact and guileless tone letting them dance together, as they do in our (human, adult) experience before abstract thought fences them off.

I remember that I have to use my head for a pencil, but it wasn't for me it was for my brother. His point broke and he sharpened my head. I was scared please.
  —*Charito, 3rd*

I remember I was watering my flowers and suddenly something came to my mind and it was a poem—it began like this: I remember flowers to dawn and dawn to night, whisper a secret and they shall fight—love isn't easy for two flowers or one whisper, blow two to one, heart to hearts, flowers as one.
  —*Mary Rodgers, 6th*

I remember when I was three years old I went to the park and I touched a squirrel.
I remember when I was little and I saw the first snow that fell, I thought it was God punishing me.
  —*Myra Guerrero, 6th*

I remember my dogs looking at me with a crazy look.
  —*Bobby Miranda, 4th*

I remember when I went to the movies with my mother and I went to the screen and everybody saw my shadow.
  —*Charles Lopez, 4th*

I remember my friend was in the door and someone put his hand on my friend's shoulder and she threw him over. It was a dog.
  —*Rosa Maria Villar, 5th*

I remember when I was born I didn't want anyone to see me.
  —*Anonymous, 3rd*

I remember when I had a bloody nose. I looked like a disgusting rose.
  —*Ahmed Kandiel, 3rd*

I remember when I went to the movie with my friend. I thought it would happen to me the next day.
  —*Meredith, 5th*

I remember I went to the movie and the picture jumped out of my mind.
I remember I saw the eyes were round going out of the moon.
I remember I made the first song, to, to, to, and the train went over me.
I remember I went to the running cars, I saw the cars going so fast my breath jumped away.
I remember I saw my brother throw his eyes at me.
  —*Guy Sancio, 6th*

I remember the day I was little and asked my mother to buy me some candy and she said she didn't have any money so I asked her to buy some money.
  —*Anonymous, 3rd*

I remember when my dog fell off the roof with a smile.
  —*Pedro Fonseca, 5th*

I

Remember
Eating a
Mushroom during an
Eclipse with
Millions of
Beautiful
Erotic men
Roaming around me.
    —*Tiffany Benn, 5th*

I remember when my dog Lady got hit by a car three times and
didn't die, but the fourth time she did.
    —*Tina Burke, 3rd*

I remember the first time I tried to write in script it looked like
buried mountains.
    —*Joseph Fernandez, 5th*

I remember smacking my face for a laughing case.
I remember my first cat. He was so white I forgot he was there.
    —*Maria Saona, 3rd*

I remember when I was one I opened my eyes and saw
  dinosaurs.
I remember when I saw the first rain I thought it was a tidal
  wave.
I remember when I was five I went to the movies and saw a
  horse. I wanted to jump on it but I broke the screen.
I remember when there was a fire in the house next door. I
  went next door and made a friend with the fire monster.
I remember when I went to the woods and saw an elephant.
  He still remembers the bloody nose I gave him.
    —*Sanjay, 3rd*

This last poem shows good skill and effort for a third grader, but the imagination is mostly programmatic and blunt. A couple of items are derived from I
Remember's read aloud. There is no ambiguity, no turn of phrase beyond the
ordinary. The elephant "remembering" a bloody nose shows some cleverness,
but at this point the student clearly lacks confidence in his own imagination
and has not developed an "ear." This can be helped by such language-oriented
assignments as lunes and acrostics.

  The following pieces have in common strong, deliberately formal elements.

DUDE RANCH

I remember horses so awesome they reached the sky.
I remember brown hunks of weathered wood.
I remember bright trees overflowing with leaves.
I remember a swimming pool reflecting sunlight.
I remember mess halls gleaming with silverware.
    —*Denise Smith, 5th*

An adult-like skill with image and metaphor. The trail of image is inspired: size coming down to natural fact, then three lights: trees/water/silverware.

> I remember when I took a banana and splashed it on my head.
> —Joann Cruz, 5th

Exaggeration ("splashed") pulls the reluctant mind's eye to fact.

> I remember what I didn't remember, something I had to
> remember after
> I remember something that I had remembered, but now, as I
> said,
> I remember everything I had to remember, but I don't want to
> remember, because
> I remember something that happened to me when
> I remember what I remember now.
> —Anonymous, 5th

Play done with remarkable control *against* a too-easy flow, leading to rhythm variety.

> I remember going camping in the woods near a pond and find-
> ing a beautiful orange salamander.
> I remember when my sister "overloved" the salamander. It
> died from being rubbed in dry sand. She cried for three days.
> I remember going to the wedding in my best pink-ruffled party
> dress and dropping the mocha-choca-chip ice cream on the
> beautiful dress.
> I remember when I wrote my name clearly for the first time.
> —Naomi Bornar, 6th

Literary details (too-pat "orange," "overloved"—drawing attention to the conventionally witty mind) leach the believability, but skill in the rapid presentation of party facts and in the word "clearly" are poetic.

> I remember when I was seven looking at the rocks and then at
> heaven.
> —Alicia, 5th

The "looking" (which stands out in the rhythm of the line) goes from something hard and "real" to a spiritual vision in an instant, and we connect rocks and heaven in our minds. The rhyme helps create a song-like flow that enables these contrasting elements to merge.

> I remember when hope was a strain beyond your strength that
> adds an inch to your inward length. Hope is the moment when
> you jump up from the trouble out of the slump. Hope is the light
> in the awful dark, the clear bright blazing becking spark that sets
> your feet to a running place for one little look at her beaking face.
> —Reynaldo Camilo, 5th

Wild and subjective, creativity too strong for a given form, rushes right through it, slightly out of whack ("becking" and "beaking"). Although the out-of-whack-ness really lies more in the *force* with which light and dark and trouble and all are subjected to the desires of the poet than in that one little various word (which could be a mistake for "beckoning").

Chapter III

TALKING TO TALKING CREATURES

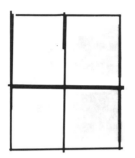

"Snake! Skin of water./ Eyes like gold."

I base one exercise on Kenneth Koch's recommendation in *Rose, Where Did You Get That Red?* I read and talk about William Blake's "The Tyger," with its magical beginning couplet "Tyger! Tyger! burning bright/ In the forests of the night," which is essentially an addressing of mythic qualities in real life. Animals are wonderful vehicles for these qualities. I also read aloud and comment on a number of children's poems based on the "Tyger" idea. I tell the kids that they don't have to try to follow Blake's rhyme-and-meter scheme. I suggest they can have the animal answer back, have a conversation. A sort of "Oh Unicorn! Oh Unicorn!" bardic flourish crops up frequently, but the best poems draw on a full range of possible poetic touches.

> Horse, Horse, clickety-clackety.
> In the ponds, splash, splash.
> Come in for a nice delight and wake yourself from the night.
> Kid, Kid, I don't have the time. But away went the horse with
>   his clickety-clackety splash splash.
>   —*Doris Norris, 5th*

Picturing (and hearing) the horse galloping through nocturnal ponds shows it to be a night-mare. The exhortation "wake yourself from the night" suggests sleep-galloping has taken place. Additional charms are the wording of "nice delight," the lone rhyme (delight/night) tucked in the middle, as if to further lyricize the nice invitation, and the horse's surprisingly Runyonesque reply.

> Lion Lion, what big eyes through
> the forest, up in the sky.
> From the mountains to the isle.
> Oh Lion what so lies? From my eyes to my bone I shiver and tiver
> with my eyes. I sit and wonder where I am. I come as your sign.

Why so high? You sit beside me. I wonder why. I like you. You
like me, so step outside and rumblewise. I fight you so you fight
me, but sometimes I wonder why. My mother comes, she smacks
you fast.
—*Ana Maria Mendez, 4th*

Surreal joie de vivre. I get a feeling of a young Emily Dickinson growing up in the
ghetto. The big eyes roam into never-never land, and it may be that the un-
familiarity with the language is the sort of detachment that lets the poet here
achieve a soulful strangeness some grownup writers make themselves sick to get
to. Note the many long i's, perhaps inspired by the first two lines of "The
Tyger." She may have decided their enchantment lay partly in that vowel.

Condor! Condor! up in the sky,
how can you fly so high?
Glowing eyes in the night.
Why do they glow like a G.E. light?
The wings of Paradise stretch so far,
why do they look like a glob of tar?
You live so high on the mountain peaks
just sitting there for twenty weeks.
—*Charles Amorosa, 4th*

Funny, through extravagant justaposition of glorious and mundane. A playful
flipping apart of the linkage rhyme brings.

As the weasel whips through
the wind he picks up a chicken.
After he finishes it he thunders
back for more.
With his beady little eyes he
watches as the chickens go by,
waiting for the right moment to attack.
What a fearless beast he is.
Very slowly he squirms by you
and you don't even know it.
—*Rita Sansotta, 4th*

Such verbs as "whips," "thunders," and "squirms" specialize the weasel's
energy. Very often kids, when they're not copying the dull adult idea of ending
a poem by summing it "up" into a thought, have an uncanny sense of the
spiritual punchiness possible in the last line, and this is a fine example. But the
poet has wisely used (luckily possessed) an adult-like breadth of vocabulary.

Whale! Whale! You're a giant
fish, your mouth is big and dark.
Your teeth are like iron, your eyes
are like shadow. Your nose is like
giant stars.
—*Alex Tsukernik, 4th*

Noticing one thing just right. Perfect economy (here mostly monosyllables), as so often, makes for impeccable sound. The line-breaks are good — the first "giant" by itself a moment lets the meaning shift with "fish"; the "shadow" comparison broken in half fits the duality; the "giant stars" twinkle a bit more because they're isolated at the end.

> Snake! Skin of water.
> Eyes like gold.
> No feet and far to go.
> To go to pits of death.
> To eat up people.
> —*Anonymous, 3rd*

First two lines a lovely, scary pair of images, followed by a witty but compassionate motto. Last two lines probably don't succeed, damage the delicacy established in the first three.

> Hi, Great White Shark. Your fin
> is like the tooth of raging
> vampire. Your mouth is like an
> opening door. Your eye is like
> the cold, dark sky, and your nose
> is like a never-ending pit.
> —*Anthony Fraticell, 6th*

Images! Perfect sharky similes for that peculiar, deadly, primal, ultimate uncaring the shark seems to corporealize. The odd "Hi" casts a slight light of whimsy without reducing the images' power.

> Oh Cheetah, Oh Cheetah,
> How do you run so fast? When you
> run, we only see a shadow cast
> upon us.
> You fly or run.
> You run so fast you're gone
> before we can say, "Look at that."
> —*Anonymous, 4th*

Three beautiful ways to express speed organically, to wit: invisibility (except of the shadow!), possibility of flight, and the cheetah's speed across the whole range of vision being faster than a breath of exclamation.

BABY BEAST

> A beast is born with
> beautiful wings.
> When he grows up
> he'll be a king.
> He has Very blue
> Eyes and very black
> hair, with colorful wings

I see right
there. He's in
his cradle so
quiet, without
sound.
                —*Belinda Aristy, 6th*

In the title a dichotomy of tone begins and is carried throughout the poem—
beauty and the beast in one creature. The silence at the end is perfect ambiguity, specifically including possibilities of the ominous and/or the innocent.

Raven, Raven, why are you so fearsome
with your three-foot long wings and
your long slickery beak so bright
in the trees of night? Don't you wish
you could be immortal? I don't know,
said the raven. I guess it's beauty sleep.
                —*Jorge Acosta, 6th*

Excellent made-up word "slickery." First the raven is pictured: size, darkness,
fierceness (beak). Romantic, spooky setting. Then the oddness of the question,
altogether surprising yet appropriate because the image we've been given suggests the timeliness of fairy tale. The "I don't know" sets up a meditative approach to the answer, then the beautiful answer, in which the raven speaks not
of his wish but of the nature of immortality. "Beauty sleep" seems to be cosmic
wit—for what possible appearance subsequent to forever would one be gather-
ing one's beauty? In any case, it's a nice shock of time-change from "immortal."

Bear, Bear, good morning, good morning, how are you today?
How are you feeling, Carmen?
I am feeling a little fine. Today is a nice day, Mr. Bear.
Yeah, a very nice day to eat you up.
Oh no, folks, a bear is going to eat me up, help help *please*.
Oh no, wait, I got a great idea. I'll hide in this cave and he will
    never get me. That silly old bear.
                —*Carmen Vega, 5th*

Perky. "A little fine" is a perfect charm, as is the sudden addressing of the audience, "Oh no, folks," heightening the theatrical up-down of feelings.
However, the tone sounds disingenuously cute, derivative.

Eel, Eel, where did you get your slimy body?
Eel, Eel, where did you get your electricity?
And where did you get your green color?
And your small eyes?
Little girl, I got my slime from the seaweed that floats in the sea.
And my electricity from thunderbolts that come from the sky.
And my green color comes from the grass where I was formed.
And my small eyes come from tiny rocks in the ground.
                —*Yvonne Rijos, 8th*

Adult-like skill serving a childlike vision. The gradual reduction of the formal elements of the questions is graceful and mature. The answers are quiet and lovely, magical but not fantastical. Reasonable, if creatures are derived from their environs.

> Lion, Lion, why are you
> King of the Jungle?
> I am King of the Jungle
> 'cause I am brave.
> Butterfly, Butterfly,
> why do you have so beautiful wings?
> I don't know, said the butterfly.
> —*Barbara, 4th*

Provocative philosophy, done, as it should (usually) be done in poetry, by implication. One "knows" reasons for kingship but not for beauty. It's also funny, the "clunk" (last line) of unpretentious truth.

> Oh little cat, why are you so
> gentle and kind? Oh little dog,
> why are you so fierce and angry?
> Oh why are *you* so white and soft?
> Oh why are you so big and small?
> I asked my animals one day. They
> just stood there watching me and then walked away.
> —*Michele Campis, 6th*

Peaceable kingdom, apparently excluding man for his uncool inquisitiveness. This may be a parody on "The Tyger" and on the assignment. Occasional rhyme (at the end) scores again.

> Tiger as a bear Tiger
> falling cats and dogs, bi
> pinga bi pinga bi binga.
> Jinga ginga inka.
> A fox in a box going to the
> socks and be be fingers, with
> butter finger binger stinker,
> butter apples staying, running
> over the moon, jump over
> the fence eating little bits
> glowing brite lite little
> mice, gaze and eat his face
> into the cheese looking into
> ears iny miny mieny mo finger
> kings butter finger butter inker
> butter stinker other men raining
> cats and dogs and the boy ran away.
> —*Sirremus Robinson, 2nd*

This is the way this second-grader wanted to bop from "Tiger," subjective goofus with a very slight bow to the animals. Good whimsical energy barely stuffed into language.

> Hi, Dog, how are you today? (I'm just
> fine.) Have you
> been after cats again?
> I heard that
> the fruit man's cart got
> knocked over today.
> —*Rebecca Benn, 4th*

Well paced, with lively fragmented line-breaks contrasting with the reasonable syntax. There is, however, something artificial in the tone of the conclusion.

> The falcon soaring through the night
> With its wings flapping fast.
> When it's in a good mood it's gentle
> But when it's enraged, Watch out.
> The falcon flies fast as the wind,
> And swoops down like a star from the sky,
> Then when it catches its prey,
> It eats it very fast and then it
> Swishes back up in the sky. With
> Its colorful colors of red, brown, white and
> Yellow it looks like a shooting star again
> Shooting upward. It looks like a
> Colorful comet coming to another part
> Of Earth.
> —*Adam Paris, 4th*

Child energy filling adult-like vocabulary range. The four colors chosen make a unified warm picture. Good verbs (soaring, flapping, flies, swoops, catches, swishes, shooting).

> A lizard is not so harmful. But if you try to put him in a fishbowl
> with fish and other lizards he will try to get out and crawl
> around your house and when you go to sweep you will see a big
> piece of dirt on the floor but it will be the lizard crawling around.
> But don't yell! Call your husband.
> —*Sojourna Thompson, 5th*

Striking tone shifts after "see" and then after each remaining phrase, from explanation to a fine, restrained metaphor ("big piece of dirt on the floor") — "crawling" to broad domestic humor.

> Dragon, where did you get those red eyes? Where did you get
> that funny messed-up nose? How did you get that fire-breathing
> mouth? Who gave you that bumpy back? How did you get that
> long tail? When did you get those pointy fingernails? Who gave
> you those funny feet? Where did you get those funny legs from?
> Where did you get that bumpy stomach?
> I got those red eyes from a brave knight. I got the nose from a

26

wicked old witch. I got the mouth from cat blood. I got the
bumpy back when the sun burned it. I got the tail from my
mother. I got the fingernails from lava in a volcano. I got those
funny feet from a Warlock. I got the legs from a statue. I got the
bumpy stomach from *you.*
　　—*Herbert Brown, 4th*

All-out. A very mixed, particular creature. The "*you*" at the end brings the
poem back from playful excess, so the dragon doesn't just seem spread out on
an enormous anatomy table.

> Leopard, leopard, fast and quick,
> you make me think you have wings
> because of the way you leap.
> Some of your fur is golden as the sun
> and your black spots are like big holes in you.
> You are graceful as a swan
> and fierce as a lion.
> If the lion wasn't the king of beasts,
> could you be?
> 　　—*William Best, 6th*

A variety of figures, as if the leopard were being looked at by a variety of eyes,
and then the touchingly cautious question "could you be?" bringing them ten-
tatively together by unifying the poem.

> Hey Cheetah, why do you run so
> fast? Why do you have black dots?
> Why do you kill other animals? Why
> don't you eat fish like the bear?
> Because that is the way nature raised me.
> Aw foowy, you don't have to kill; you
> can eat grass or fish like I told you.
> You're just stubborn, that's all.
> "Gulp," said the
> cheetah and that was the end of me.
> 　　—*Jamahl Sheppard, 4th*

Quick narrative of how the irritatingly persistent hubris of man may call
Nature down upon itself.

　The "Tyger" assignment helps the kids write because it has a simple, built-in
structure: question and answer, which gives them a feeling for form, a
shapeliness, always satisfying in art. But because of its freedom the form is
flexible enough to be alive for them.

Chapter IV

THE CHANT

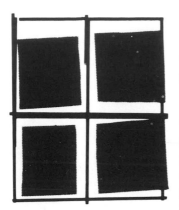

"When I look into the light I see the nice blue waters moving to a rhythmic beat"

The chant, which for teaching purposes I take to be the repetition of some fixed phraseology juxtaposed within each line of the poem with changing material, must be one of the oldest poetic forms, preliterate plus. Probably, in fact, the very beginning: repetitive sounds, then words, accompanying ceremonial dance and music. It affords students a chance to have structure and freedom so close they breathe on each other. The juxtapositions can amount to graceful, humorous, comprehensive "graphs" of experience. A very formal situation like this points up the possibility of locating the power of the poem, by emphasis, in very specific places.

> People Look people
> people how people
> people many people
> people times people
> people I people
> people told people
> people this people
> people stupid people
> people person people
> people to people
> people say people
> people people people.
> —*Eylin Velez, 8th*

Many times, given a formal lead, students will invent striking techniques: this is to be read down as well as across. The chant rhythm here flourishes because kids don't get self-conscious about repetition.

> When I go to sleep
> my eyes close my mouth
> opens my feet go to
> sleep my stomach starts
> growling and my whole
> body gets tender.

When
I wake up my eyes
open my mouth closes
my feet awaken my
stomach stops growling
and my whole body gets
very hard
      and then
when I go outside
my body gets cold
and I get the chillbumps.
      —*Marc Edwards, 5th*

The highlight of this original piece is the tender/hard metamorphosis, a beautiful exaggeration of a sensitive awareness. The "chillbumps" seems to mock that dichotomy.

Yes it is
Yes it would
Yes you could
Yes I will
Yes I am
Yes it is
Yes you should
Yes it will
Yes she will
Yes it can
Yes she is
Yes I do, and I love you.
      —*Anonymous, 3rd*

This repetition leads to abstraction, warmed a little by the affirmative, which then bursts out tenderly in the last line—a surprise but set up (by the positive tone of the "yes's") too.

When I opened the map it turned.
When I opened the map lights were on.
When I opened the map people were popping out.
When I opened the map I was sucked in.
      —*Ramsey Monagro, 3rd*

The inanimate animated. The choices, except for people popping perhaps, are excellent — motion/light/union. A very close encounter, zooming in on a microcosm rather than expanding into space.

Green flame, people, paper,
green flags, boards, tables, animals, fur.
green hair, food, teeth,
green clocks, apples, pies, clothes, beans,
green books, rings, words,
green nails, chairs, bottoms, kings, stars.
      —*Rowe, 4th*

Excellent variation in the occurrences of "green" and (thus) the line-lengths, also in the possible greenness of the things mentioned. The reader can be absorbed in the gradual erratic stretching to breaking-point of his faith in what can be green, a rhythm of idea, and at the same time feel the overlapping physical rhythm of sound. A regularity lies in the 3-5-3-5-3-5 pattern, line by line, of the "things."

> My mother went to Hawaii.
> My father went to the moon.
> My brother went crazy.
> My grandmother went home.
> My friend went bonkers.
> My uncle went to Florida.
> My teacher went on a vacation.
> I wish my cousin went to Jupiter.
> My car went to the junkyard.
> My aunt went to Washington.
> I went to bed.
> —*Chi Man Leung, 5th*

Double variation each line, plus variation irregularly throughout between "real" and fantastic. Nice downbeat ending, upbeat in actual effect via its contrast. Since the repeated material is only one single word ("went") and the variation so abundant, the poem is as much a list poem as a chant. The emphasis is much more on the changes than on the repetition.

> Sing me a song.
> Sing me a lot.
> Sing me so much that the ceiling will fall.
> Sing me so much that the building will fall.
> Sing with a horrible voice.
> Sing, sing, sing, so it can ring, ring, ring.
> —*Elizabeth Delerm, 5th*

The progression in pairs, "song"/"a lot," "ceiling"/"building" and the last pair (which divides again in the last line) is expansive in three different ways: from thing to-number, part to whole, oddity ("horrible voice") to "ring, ring, ring" (growth). This all seems harmonious with the idea of "song."

> I like math.
> You like math.
> The dog likes math.
> The cat likes math.
> The rabbit likes math.
> The wind is blowing.
> The wind likes math.
> We like math.
> The earth likes math.
> The door likes math.
> There is a hole in the sky.

The hole likes math.
My math book likes math.
The floor in the house likes math.
People like math.
The word math likes math.
The sentence likes math.
The fractions like math.
The galaxy likes math.
The moon likes math.
The spaceman likes math.
The comets like math.
The meteors like math.
The telescope likes math.
Mars likes math.
The sun likes math.
The numerator likes math.
The flashlight likes math.
The axis likes math.
        —*Ronald McKune, 4th*

The chief attractions here are, again, the surprise-laden variations in the *types* of each new thing mentioned, and, especially, the choice of "math," which does relate in interesting ways to anything drawn to it. In the section from "galaxy" through "meteors" (or perhaps through "numerator") there is not enough differentiation, however.

I live in a house with you.
I like it too.
I wish I could always see you.
I like it, it's cool.
I want to see you every day.
I want you.
I'll keep you.
I'll not dare trade you.
I like you the way you are.
I'll read to you.
I'll do anything you say.
I want to keep you but I can't.
I wish I could know you.
I wish I was a princess.
I wish it was true.
I would miss you if you left.
I'd like that too.
I like you.
        —*Jackie Lee, 3rd*

Bold amount of variation in the form, breaking the given "rule" really (as many of the best kids' poems do). It holds up though, as sufficient repetition to balance repetition against change. The lines have much natural-speech energy.

I studied for my spelling test.
I studied for my math test.
I studied how many times my brother got sick.
I studied how many chicken pox Dawn has.
I studied how the dog barks.
I studied how the cat turns his head.
I studied the stickers in my album.
I studied my own voice.
I studied my own birthday.
I studied my brother's birthday.
I studied my classroom.
I studied my name.
I even studied who I am.
But I still didn't study
how much 300 divided by five is. I think it is 3.
        —*Olga Katznelson, 3rd*

Subtle progression outward from expectable studies. The "cat turns his head"
is a beautiful step along the way. The meaning of "study" deepens as we go in
this poem. Joke at the end doesn't help much.

Travel to a hotel.
Travel to an aquarium.
Travel on a ship.
Travel to a friend's house.
Travel all day.
Travel till the moon comes.
Travel till you're tired.
Travel till you're old, then
Travel to Thomas' house for champagne.
        —*Thomas Kersma, 5th*

The progression in the *view* of travel is fine—first a variety of destinations, then a
concentration on the process itself. The need for a rest becomes increasingly apparent; the "punchline" is perfect and warm, and the refreshments fancy.

Who am I?
Where do I come from?
Where am I going?
Who will I be?
Where will I live?
What will I do?
Who are my friends?
Who understands me?
Who is God?
Where is God?
What is hope?
What is knowledge?
Where is my imagination?
Where will I be?

> Who will I love?
> When will I die?
> Why do I care?
>   —*Jane Martinez, 8th*

This eighth grade girl, who wrote some wonderfully jagged, sincere acrostics, is here, though using a bold formal variation (repeated use of the question form rather than of key words), caught in an over-literary series. Once the reader catches on to the *type* of variation, there are no more surprises; the progression is stiff, thus doesn't progress. Not nearly as supple as the similarly made chant by third grader Jackie Lee (above).

> Come home, I cried today.
> Come home, it's awful dark.
> Come home, the clouds look mean.
> Come home, the trees block paths.
> Come home before the morning
> lights so many paths to go.
>   —*Marilyn Alameda, 6th*

Unabashed lyric. The formal element keeps the sentiment in proportion, a real song even without music. The last "come home" stretches out nicely.

> One morning I woke up and I woke up my mother, my mother woke up my father, my father woke up my grandmother, my grandmother woke up my grandfather, my grandfather woke up the house beside our house, the house beside our house woke up the neighbor, the neighbor woke up the other neighbor, the other neighbor woke up Manhattan, Manhattan woke up Queens, Queens woke up Brooklyn, Brooklyn woke up 42nd St., 42nd St. woke up Mexico, Mexico woke up Canada, Canada woke up Pennsylvania, Pennsylvania woke up the hole world, the hole world woke up the other planets.
>   —*Ramira Honeywell, 4th*

Wonderful stutter-step (tiny moves "outward" interspersed with sudden huge ones) but lustily expansive progression.

> I won't do it—
> go to school
> I won't do it—what I'm supposed to do
> I won't do it
> Ah - Ah - Ah
> I won't do it
> I just won't.
>   —*Aaron Taylor, 6th*

Impishness made jazzy by live speech rhythms.

> Me and my friend we go so great.
> Me and my friend eat off the same plate.
> Me and my friend tell each other we're nice.
> Me and my friend say that every day twice.
>   —*Angelina Tucker, 6th*

The rhythm in connection with the rhyme acts like Ogden Nash poems do (without the exaggerated line lengths). The wry self-deprecation ("we're nice," "we're nice"), clear of any qualifying tint, is a child specialty. That is, there's a freedom from self-consciousness here. Adult poems of self-deprecation typically carry an unspoken current of "I'm really above this" or else a sadly settled "I hate my life." The colloquial "we" in line 1 helps the tone and the rhythm.

> When I opened the refrigerator a giant red tomato jumped on
>   me.
> When I opened the refrigerator a carrot threw carrot juice at
>   me.
> When I opened the refrigerator a glob of jello flew on me.
> When I opened the refrigerator a drumstick beat on my head.
> When I opened the refrigerator rice started shooting at me.
> When I opened the refrigerator the soup fell on my feet.
> The next time I go in that refrigerator, I'm carrying a gun.
>   —John Russell, 6th

Obvious sort of imagination works well here, mainly due to the variation in type of attack and the unabashed broadness of the tone.

> When I look into the light I see dancing girls doing a marathon
>   dance.
> When I look into the light I see brightness & darkness.
> When I look into the light I see the gentle fast movement of
>   the light.
> When I look into the light I see the electricity passing through
>   the lines to the light.
> When I look into the light I see a crispy sharp look.
> When I look into the light I see the nice blue waters moving to
>   a rhythmic beat.
> When I look into the light the light is talking to me.
> When I look into the light it's telling me, "Look, smell the
>   rhythm."
> When I look into the light it smells delicious & sweet, inno-
>   cent & harmless.
>   —Anonymous, 5th

A large, primal vision is partly developed here, out of an everyday optical fact. Synesthesia at the end. The order of the elements seems a bit scattered, but each line is a powerful attempt to record exactly what's seen, whether "illu-sion" or empirical fact.

> Twigs I see in the skies.
> Twigs, they melt in my mind.
> Twigs I see in your eyes.
> Twigs I see on the side.
> Twigs I see in your mind.
> Twigs twigs twigs twigs
> are on my mind.
>   —Maribell Esteves, 5th

The lovely oddity of choosing twigs, along with the emphasized linear shape and branchiness of twigs, leads to symbolic thought. Twigs might evoke various impressions in the reader's mind — a thickety quality in nature or in general, something above us, linearity. When we study the poem we may get glimmers of these senses. But (quite properly) we don't get them too directly or too easily, due to such inspired phrases as "melt in my mind" and "see on the side." In other words, a nice balance of expansion and obstacle hovers around the twig idea.

> I think and I see ice cream melting.
> I think and I see my dog go for a bone.
> I think and planes land on my building.
> I think and my mother is playing baseball.
> I think and the moon comes out.
> I think and turkey is on my bed.
> I think and fruits are in my ear.
> I think and spring is here.
> That's why I think so much.
> —*Kevin Rivera, 4th*

What begins as a look-around piece becomes, by repetition and by little moves away from the limitations of "real" detail, an illustration of the power of thought. Last line clicks any remaining doubts away.

> I think of you
> I think of me
> I think of everything this world can be
> I think of sunlight
> I think of rain
> I think I'm going insane
> I think of flowers
> I think of thorns
> I think of animals with pointed horns
> I think of the beginning
> I think of the end
> and this is what I think I'll send.
> —*Leara Bowles, 5th*

Fine multi-form piece (chant, rhyme, regularity of line-length variation) done, as all these poems are, in twelve to fifteen minutes in the classroom hurly-burly and without time to reflect on structure. Very strong link between thought and concrete image (for example, the parallel thrusts of sunlight-rain-insane and flowers-thorns-horns).

> She is my friend.
> She is like me.
> She is like the breeze that runs through the sea.
> She is so nice.
> She is not like ice.
> She is as soft as a cotton ball.

She is not tall.
She is so smart.
She broke my heart.
—*Caroline Gardenas, 5th*

Formally inspired by Leara Bowles' poem (above). The "punchline" is excellent, due to the twin powers (here) of rhyme and surprise—the linking power of rhyme bridges a large gap, with suspension and no suspense. The irregular line-lengths keep the rhymes from being singsongy.

Listen to the rooster crow in the morning.
Listen to the feet creeping along the floor.
Listen to the pancake frying nice and brown.
Listen to the way you talk and sound.
Listen to the water running in the tub.
Listen to your dog barking for grub.
Listen to all the people you meet.
Listen to your snoring when you're asleep.
Listen to the kids talking in school.
Listen to the teachers who holler at the kids.
Listen to the sun rise at dawn.
Listen to the heartbeat of a bug.
Listen to the mice running for cheese.
Listen to the cool breeze.
—*Korie Powell, 6th*

A progression from clear-cut physical hearing inward to what can be listened to only in thought and spirit. But the progression is not smooth, which is good because that would reduce the details to mere illustrations of the idea's movement. Likewise the on-and-off rhyme works fine, relates to the listen idea, sharpens attention via the uneven progress of aural image.

The sun is funny.
The sun is blue.
The sun is purple.
The sun is crazy.
The sun is bright.
The sun is good.
The sun is strong.
The sun is hot.
The sun is mighty fine.
The sun is amusing.
The sun is wonderful.
The sun is pretty good.
The sun is going to fall down.
—*Peter Cerreta, 2nd*

A second-grader mixes ordinary, fantastic, and colloquial sun characterizations in a very simple format, leaving the basic graph of the poem's images thus unadorned. Most of the entries, as they come in line, have surprise impact, especially "mighty fine," "pretty good," and "going to fall down."

Chapter V

WRITING TOGETHER

"instructing the sun/ is easy with my hands"

I've found the cluster of forms known as collaborations to be extremely fruitful, especially as training. Due to the continual trade-offs in the compositional method, the burden of intentionality is lifted. Writing together, we tend to concentrate on finding a common language to speak rather than on making a point. The absence of purpose tends to fill with association and response. Fragmentation of story and sense encourages a focus on syntax as play—a big attitudinal step toward mastery.

> I have seen
> the tree on the corner
> in a spring bud
> and summer green
> yesterday
> it was yellow gold
> then a cold wind began to blow
> now I know you really don't see a tree
> until you don't see its bones.
> —*Tamara D. & Yvonne Luna, 7th*

Here the "moves" resemble those of a contemporary adult poem. The sounds of "seen" are caught again in "tree on the corner/ in a spring" and "summer green." "Yesterday," "yellow," "gold," "cold," "began," "blow," "know," "see," "tree," "bones," and others keep up a thread of graceful echoes throughout. The line-breaks help establish a supple rhythm. The o's blowing through the last four lines harmonize with the bone thought. "Yellow gold" stands out in the spare, quick language of the poem.

THE MOON—IT'S A BUSY PLACE

Stars walking all over.
Working hard to shine.

Who still after years get very little
pay. But they get a day off to watch
their favorite program *The Jetsons*
and afterwards go out to light and
play with their pals, but all of a
sudden bang boom pop poop a little
star with her star-pox who got sick
and wants to find out from what, so
she goes to the doctor and finds out
she's allergic to the moon.
                    —*Estella Pando & Maritza Rodrigues, 7th*

Astral anthropomorphism, a little loony charm.

●

I have often made collaborative poems with my own children, using any
number of simple methods. For the following piece my daughter Sierra (age
nine) and I wrote alternating lines and I end-rhymed my lines to hers.

Once when I was a little squirt
& everything was wonderful & everything hurt,
I went over to the big brown chair
to sit me down in its comfortable air.
While I was sitting I saw a paw
creep in the door, so brown & raw.
It had no body, it had no bones,
behind it oozed some ghostly moans.
It was the year of 2001,
a strange new age had just begun.
When the paw came closer
I screamed, "No sir!
You can't do that
like some vampire bat!"
I took out the TV plug
& threw it at this spooky lug.
Suddenly it exploded—
apparently it was loaded.
Those ghostly moans
rose to human tones.
Apparently it was my father,
so why bother?
I got so mad
at that Halloween dad
that suddenly I went aboard
his shoulders with a silver sword.
I killed that daddy of mine
because he was way too fine.

Although an immediate draw here is the "cleverness" of the rhymes, it can be
seen by running down the poem alternately that the poetic feeling resides in

her lines. I've found, collaborating with kids, that it's best to act modestly, just clean up a little and be poetic straight-man.

The following acrostic was made by me and my son Franz, then fourteen.

SHAMPOO

She washed her
Hair
And
Made it look
Pretty as
Orange blossoms
Of the East.

The tradeoff was done line by line and fell in place with the neatness of a unilateral piece.

The following poem was also done in alternating lines; my partner was Chris Collom, then seven or eight. Chris' lines are in italics.

INSTRUCTING THE SUN

is easy with my hands
to invade the earth below
and get us too hot
to remind us of years ago
when the dazzling faraway light
came to a rewarding
gold bars dropped in it
three books stick together
& when you read them all at once
they dazzle away
I signalled that to the sun
with blood instructors away
making animals in the pool
to rise from high to low
being more proper for the sun
as you read below it
in the middle of the night
to question mark the ways
we also follow: circles
& scatter around
the ways so short they don't curve
like an h growing up
to an H
as I wonder around
behind it to get speech
& speed up around it
until talk is a circle
to quarterback the ways
my hands can wave the sun around
& speech goes away

in space
as we go
trying to tell it what
the H is rumbling for

In this and other poems made with Chris at that age, I felt that he was the fount of quicksilvery energy, composing rings around me, that my own responses when not sufficiently humble evinced a deleterious stodginess. His main advantage was an ability to make leaps, large or small, that transcended any expectable logic but were ex post facto made of feeling.

I wrote the following two pieces with Franz (fourteen) and Sierra (six) respectively in New York City, alternating lines.

The lines of Charlie's painting are waving around on
blood-red skies
with a touch of blue.
As I think, I sniff wandering air
and the night dims over the crusty city.
Points of light open their arms
in the dark sky.
Charlie trips on a broken sidewalk,
lands on his you-know-what
and catches a new line of thought.
— Four shots we thought firecrackers
and a man lies dead on Ludlow.
We rush to the window.

●

I went to the store one day and bought some fish
a drink, whereupon they told me of the Lost Treasure.
The fish told me also about raisins
and dried water, to carry over the Orange Desert.
Dried water is like some pieces of band-aids
on a star. Well, I started out for the Lost Treasure,
but a big wedding dress came to me
and started to choke me. Oof,
ping-pong-ball played itself under the ocean.
"Where was the Treasure?!"
I decided to say. It took me an hour to decide.
The phone rang. "Hi Treasure here. Come find me.
I'm about two blocks away. Operator standing by."
I dashed out, ordered a hot dog & took a bite.
That big bite told me, "You are maybe going to
find the Treasure. Take another bite.
Then I'll be gone." "Oh mercy,"I said.
"Are you the Treasure, or this golden mustard?"
"I am the big Car-Wash, and that's the truth
of my story." I sat down and a little girl walked up.

The fish was gone. The fish had taken away my hair-style.
I realized that the Treasure was all around me.

Out of a feeling for documentary authenticity, I've left all of these collaborations with my children thoroughly unedited. Certain phrases cry out for revision, in a sense, but to apply anything like normal verse standards would, I
think, tend to cut out the life's blood of the poems. Their energy depends on
the shucking away of standard conventions and, as in Whitman and in fact
even in John Donne, the charm or genius is inextricably mingled with what
seem to be inexcusable excesses.

This next piece was done with Sierra Collom (at ten), in alternating words.
Such a format seems to lead to prose, albeit a totally goofy prose, rather than
the rhythms of poetry.

> What is green with long legs? asked Mr. Glasses. I said nothing. I
> didn't like this question, it's too personal, I have no good hopes
> for this green-legged study. Can a doggy. Shucks! I bought a ticket
> to Asia. Why did I do something far like that? If I had enough dog-
> gies for canning, I would stay in Alabama, but no doggies showed
> up. So I jumped off my refrigerator & didn't look down my
> sleeve at suppertime. Asia! What a doggy place! Uh-oh, though, I
> forgot my cash. Time healed fast & nobody cared whatsoever.
> Work is hard & soft if you don't know what to do. Gosh, I lived
> in Asia ten months before I lived smoothly. Ah, then I just dog-
> gied along, tongue to the wind, eating the canned shadows of
> Asia. Oops was here, my long friend. Speaking Asian, I'd express
> something half-sideways. Something brown didn't matter,
> because it's only reflection, doggy shine. Oh! Suddenly I lost my
> Oops, you see. No sunlight isn't much here in Alabama—hey, what
> is green with long legs? What? A person like this Oops said, "A
> doggy, especially a green thing, long-legged with smiles on its arm."

Such a piece is loaded to the gills with whimsy. In removing the compositional
reliance on the phrase, in forcing a singular consideration of each word, and
from the semi-alien stance of just having received a word from one's partner,
this form discharges the molecular humors of syntax. My favorite approach is
to try to be modest and sensible; due to the tight trade-offs, it's impossible to
avoid sounding crazy. When participants continually use their turns to say the
most colorful thing possible, the enterprise degenerates into a mere list of con-
volutions. The fun is in the tension between sense and departure from sense.

The following piece—not strictly a collaboration—was dictated to me by my
son Nat. I was at my desk and he, then age four, walked by. I asked him if he
wanted to make a poem and he stopped, wheeled around, and began confident-
ly calling it out, with deliberate pauses that I took down as line-breaks. Poetry
(though not this type) was "around the house" but this was his first attempt.

> I was thinking about poems
> I'm thinking about poems

a poem
I got it in my head
I got a poem in my head
now I'm thinking about a poem
I want to only say
8
8
2
2
2
8
9
4
6
and 4
and 8
6
and 4
9
6
and 4
and 8
6
2
and 1
and 8 o e e t
and 8 and 1
6 and 8
e a a o a a e o
o 4 e a t
9 and 6 and u a t
6 and 7
9 and 6
4-9
8 and t
4 and t
4 and t
8 and t
and a t 9 a t
6 and t
9 and t
40 and t
9 and 6 and t
a o o t
6 and 7 t
and 4 and t
A and a t
4 and 1 and t
6 and 7 North Street

9 and 6 and street
1 and 40 and t
boy into t
snow into t
into a t o t
4 and 9 and t
9 and 6 t
t o
and door
table
pig
lion
horsey
cowboy
and soup
pig
and I want a wagon
cowboy
glass
cup
cowboy
I'm telling all about the animals
and a horse
cowboy
and a table
pig
elephant
A

potato

syrup

pancake

If little kids have such a proclivity for rhythm and playful experimentation, perhaps something could be made of it (Poets-in-the-Nurseries?).

Chapter VI

CANDIDNESS AND INNOCENCE

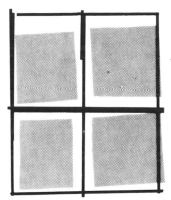

"I put my head up and let it float down"

In this chapter I've grouped poems that exhibit a sort of pure subjective realism—obviously a slippery categorization. These are poems in which the personal vision is expressed in unaffected feeling, as if the author were unaware there might be other ways to look at things. This lack of self-consciousness allows the vision its own full strength.

Some of the ways this comes (or goes) out are:

• Brags—expansions and accelerations of the sense of self, effects of the self on faraway objects.

• Informality, and how it can illuminate the formal atmospheres it enters.

• The poignance of unaffected simplicity.

• The capturing of "voices" that are genuine and consistent.

• Openness to "accidental" wisdom, cosmic or incidental ("Nothing is more beautiful than a universe").

• The happy shock of sudden, unusual juxtapositions (the sequitur-ness of nonsequiturs).

• A sensitivity (because preconceptions don't get in the way) to "ripples" all around.

• Wildness ("ya ya ya ya").

• Speech rhythm. The funny things with words, humor that goes beyond jokes.

• New ideas, including new forms.

• Speed of diction.

• Freedom of syntax, revelation of the usually repressed, stream of consciousness.

• Tension, thus energy, when candidness and innocence meet sophistication.

ACROSTICS

> East to west
> South to north,
> Train to plane,
> Running from sides and minds,
> Aching pain
> Love and hate,
> Investigating what comes to mind,
> Talking and chatting
> About what flies through the air.
> —*Estralita Brown, 6th*

An acrostic delineating the first name of the writer. Her impetus seems to be to cover a lot of space and to create a sense of acceleration upwards about herself. The first three lines limn this clearly. "Running from sides and minds" is a terrific way to undercut the portentous intentionality of the mind and class it as a set of opinions that is just there, part of the personal scene, without a sense of overriding value. "Chatting" lightens the flying things for flight. Estralita's involved in a free, "thoughtless" dance of her own verbal imagination.

> Tell me, Stars, what do you do?
> Every day?
> Let me know all the facts
> Every day. Tell me how
> School is everyday up there.
> Come on, start telling me about the
> Other stars.
> Pop up some day by my place and
> Eat some dinner.
> —*Antoine St. Louis, 5th*

The jolly warmth of the "everyday" tone of speech ropes in the faraway stars. How do you talk to a star? In a friendly, perky way, as you would to anyone you like, he seems to say, through his personal "telescope."

> Adrian ran down the road, made a
> Dent in a window and he
> Ran back home, then he was
> Inside the house. Then there was
> An assembly waiting for him.
> "No you don't," they said.
> —*Adrian Harry, 4th*

"Dent" in a window is a charm, an extravagant, guilty euphemism. You can feel the Huck Finn feet shuffling in the dust. He gives intention away with his ran-down, ran-back as if the deed were the point of the whole run. Adrian had considerable language deficiencies, yet his balance in the placements of himself —the way he sort of pops up—works cinematically; that is, the mentions of himself are placed in a visual progression. And that curt, all-wise authority-statement "No you don't" ends things quickly with a fine mix of implication and finality, the judgment. At the same time, an "assembly" at home saying that quick thing ("No you don't") is solemnly hilarious, especially when pictured.

> "Go away, I'm not your friend."
> OK, I will go away.
> Impossible, I was playing
> Now, and now he is not my friend.
> "Go away," he said.
> —*Lidia Acosta, 3rd*

Very moving. The acquiescence in line 2, the "Impossible" and the recapitulation—"'Go away,' he said"—describe an emotional trail recognizeable to us all, but not usually captured, let alone so concisely and within a form. "Going" is the perfect acrostic backbone word to express and ruefully play with the stutter-steps of perception that make up the little process of sad realization. This process is aided by the two "now's" split from each other.

> A boy is
> Lying to me.
> Oh, I
> Need the
> Excitement.
> —*John Lucas, 3rd*

For a third-grader to know, and know articulately, that it's better (except perhaps for a saint) to be lied to than be ignored is the breathtaking capsule clarity of the naive. The poem's thought is not cloyed by any principle, around which rationalizations might gather.

> Lost in a woods
> I saw a
> Girl. She was so beautiful my
> Heart was torn apart.
> The girl didn't like me as much as I liked her.
> —*Anonymous, 6th*

The first four lines are transparent and fragmented, extreme like a vision, and are contrasted to the mundane tone and structure (one sentence, one line) of the last line, to heighten the crash of his dream—but only so far: the subtlety of "not...as much" leaves the door slightly open.

PLACE POEMS

> I have a cave in the sea. It is black
> and spooky. I go there every morning and get money.
> If someone comes into it and sees me I will go crazy,
> and I love that place so much I love it at a touch.
> The water is blue.
> —*Kassinda Williams, 4th*

Striking simplicity (in context, after the initial spookiness) of "get money" and the non-sequitur "the water is blue" following swift, keen, rhyming (much/touch) insight. A quick picture. The idea of going crazy simply upon being *seen* is powerful.

CHRISTINA'S SONG

La la la la, da da da da
    do
Norway Norway ya ya Norway Norway
    ya ya
Norway, it's my favorite place
Don't you know it's good? It's
    Norway
ya ya Norway ya ya ya ya
You should go there sometime
Don't worry, the bugs won't eat you
    La la
You might think it's very spooky
    Do do do do
Ha ha ha ha
    Don't worry
Norway is still there
Watching YOU.
    —*Christina, 3rd*

Direct, unlikely, wild song. Sudden mundanities ("You should go there sometime") provide contrast, roughen it well for a more authentic charm.

A deserted farm is a lonely place.
It gives you a deep cold thought.
As the wind blows through the tall weeds
the trees bend and crackle
and the windmill squeaks
while the door claps wildly against the barn.
    —*Fred Beanblossom, 9th*

This farmboy's sincerity imparts power: the simplicity of "it gives you" followed by the quietly dramatic plunge of "a deep cold thought." That is, a more sophisticated syntax would take away emotional believability. Then he properly finds sound, paradoxically, the best impression for loneliness and makes a series that builds from a whisper (line 3) in four steps to the slamming at the end, violently poignant since there's still no one there. The word "claps" suggests applause, hands, people, which intensifies the loneliness.

LUNES

Torres is hoping
to get my girl. Ah,
he won't succeed.
    —*Robert, 7th*

Starting with "Torres" so bluntly, no first name, no description, shows the cutting away of the explanatory that the lune forces, and reveals the way he

occurs regularly in the writer's mind. No other information on Torres is needed. The "Ah" lifts the clamped-down abstract tone of the last line with an
emotional flutter.

> I am tired.
> Please don't wake me up.
> Morning isn't over.
> —*Deana C., 5th*

The economy of talk. Humor in the last line without relinquishing pace.

> I lost something.
> I am going to cry,
> probably right now.
> —*Lisa La Motta, 4th*

Cute time warp of "probably" as it fits in right "now."

> Go to the
> store and check it out.
> Buy a peach.
> —*Jesse Isaacs, 3rd*

Again, colorless (monosyllable) economy setting up (peach) epiphany, which
pops in quick as a rising sun.

> I went home,
> put on cologne and started
> to be happy.
> —*Farrah, 5th*

Almost-rhyme links and emphasizes the humor of the two happifying agents,
"home" and a dab of perfume. Cuts through lofty pretense about what makes
us happy.

> Sky is light.
> Sun will fill the air.
> You will see.
> —*Monica Grier, 5th*

You wouldn't think such simple words could express something as delicate as
the present/future overlap of the pre-dawn sun ("is light," "will fill"). The
double meaning of "see" is put with perfect concision but keeps up this feeling
of two things in one.

> I want the
> world to know that I
> am here today.
> —*Edwin M., 6th*

And now it does.

> When Kaisha goes
> the stars are closed and
> the river flows.
> —*Kaisha White, 5th*

Her boast is vast and musical.

> I am too
> gorgeous, and a lot of
> guys are satisfied.
> —*Barbara Drepaul, 6th*

"Too" gorgeous works with "satisfied" to do afresh Blake's paradox, "The road of excess leads to the palace of wisdom." "A lot of" is funnier the more you think of it. The music is clarified by the hard g alliteration and how it's positioned.

> Black is dark,
> red and yellow very bright.
> Purple is both.
> —*Brenda Tavarez, 6th*

Good, weird perception, a new color classification. "Very" fits brightness but not darkness (when it's just plain physical).

> If I could
> I would, but I can't
> so I won't.
> —*Kim Mortley, 5th*

A nifty formal hover. Tight monosyllabic rhythm and sharp *t* sounds swing it through.

> My sisters sometimes
> bother me. So what? I
> bother them back.
> —*Melissa Baez, 4th*

Perkiness preserved in perfect quotidien pace. Not a trace of deadness in the rhythm.

> A leaf is
> more soft than you ever
> thought it was.
> —*Francis Pena, 5th*

A fine choice (softness) to illustrate reality vs. thought.

THING POEMS

> Dear Floor,
>   Why don't you shout when people step on you? You're so dirty. Why don't you clean yourself? Don't you have a face? You don't have teeth because you just lay there and the people smashed them away.
> —*Nephthys Minaya, 3rd*

Here the writer makes sudden leaps (from the qualified empathy of the first sentence to the flat statement "You're so dirty," from the cleaning question to "Don't you have a face?"). Adults often labor over transitions, striving to create a smooth, logical continuum. Such a continuum may be, however, too intellectualized to show vividly the actual emotional instant-by-instant responses. A delicate combination of scorn and concern is clearly revealed in this piece, using particulars of observation and imagination, not generalization.

> My hand with five fingers sort of seems
> like a road with green grass, green
> trees and a horse galloping. All of a sudden,
> a bird chirps. Then a crowd
> of birds starts chirping together,
> and a beautiful melody comes out.
> —*Maria Perdikis, 5th*

Dramatic, matter-of-fact leap from hand to country road is followed by color, then motion (galloping horse), then sound, and it all turns to joy. Compare the progression with that of the "numbers" acrostic in the Introduction.

> The egg is like scrambles. It
> gets talk and a conversation
> on the fire. It's a team of them
> and they just move around in the
> fryer. Then it sits on the plate
> staring at me. Then I stick
> a fork in it and it looks
> sick. Then I eat and I
> feel like a killer.
> —*Kevin Burgess, 7th*

The oddities of syntax ("is like scrambles," "It gets talk," "It's a team of them") create a sense of energy, thus life, in the eggs. Altogether the eggs move, talk, organize themselves, sit, stare, and look sick when stabbed. Every observation is accurate, albeit anthropomorphized. The ending is almost too logically built-up-to; the poem's best energy is in the first half, before the idea takes over, though the penultimate sentence is good and shocking.

WILLIAM CARLOS WILLIAMS IMITATIONS

> This is just to say
> I have eaten the ice cream
> in the freezer which you were probably
> saving for your boyfriend.
> Forgive me,
> it was so cold and I was so angry.
> —*Cesar Victorino, 4th*

"Angry" and in fact the whole last line are both special, jumping out of close imitation of Williams' plum poem. Line 4 keeps to the facts in a deadly trochaic rhythm.

I am sorry I
let your
sister spill the
juice but
it looked like
orange raindrops
falling from the
sky.
                    —*Kerry Washington, 1st*

Dictated to me by a first-grader with great certainty, especially in delineating line breaks, which are musical and various (as if she'd been studying Robert Creeley). "Orange raindrops" stands out, properly, as the only smoothly rhythmic line, and "sky" is special too, the endless little end, rhyming with the beginning.

VARIOUS POEMS

Yesterday my mother bought a
dozen of eggs for breakfast and

my	brother	was	putting	them
away	and	he	dropped	them
on	the	floor	and	my
mother	wanted	me	to	make
some	eggs	for	us	then
I	asked	her	where	are
the	eggs	and	she	asked
my	brother	acted	like	he
did	not	know	what	she
was	talking	about	and	then
I	saw	some	yellow	slimy
things	on	the	floor.	

                    —*Rebecca Benn, 4th*

A new form! Amazing effect of lifting extremely mundane events into exact notice and metaphysical possibilities, symbolic rumbles. Bonus: the random charms of reading down the columns for suggestive juxtapositions in or out of the main story.

Yesterday I remember when my best friend told me that she is going to kill me. Anyway I'm alive now. And I wish I could stay that way. And I wish I could kill her because she almost stepped on my doggy.

Anyway I like her because she is my best friend and I forgive her. But still if she stepped on my doggy I would kill her and I know she would forgive me because I am her best friend.
                    —*Asya Golodets, 4th*

This might be judged merely "confused" and frighteningly so, but poetically it's true to immediate workings of the mind, not so crazy that we can't all recognize such violent contradictions in our own awarenesses.

> When I went to a Roller Skating Palace with my friend Lida Dia-
> mond she bumped into this kid and she liked him so she told me to
> ask him if he liked her so I did and he said why, does she like me
> and I said yes. So I told her. And she told me to ask him his name
> so I did. And his name was Jerry. So I told her. And she told me to
> ask him if he wanted to skate with her so he asked her. And she
> said no. Then he asked me and I said no. Then we left.
> —*Anonymous, 4th*

Monosyllables roll unpunctuated for awhile, pulling attention to the grayness
of the speech, so "Jerry" jumps out like a cherry. Taken to a funny extreme
with a perfect deadly downer end. Should be required reading for every boy,
against a sensitive hubris (rejections is not necessarily rejection of *you*).

> One day we were going
>   to get something we wanted.
> My brother got socks,
> my sisters got something.
> I went outside and got
> me a little blue parakeet.
> When I brought him home
> everybody talked to him
> and they forgot all
> about me.
> —*Lefebvre Lockley, 6th*

Paradigm of the tragedy of satisfied desire; poignant through clear fact alone.
"Little blue" is attractive. "Outside" too, as if blue parakeets "grew on trees,"
and the me of "got me" is a nice colloquial touch, the only ungrammatical usage
in the poem. It stands out further via the line-break.

> -------my hand is light.
> -------how did I know?
> -------because I lift it.
> -------every day some
> -------time I look at my hand
> -------and say wow
> -------look at my pinky
> -------so small and skinny
> -------with a silver ring
> -------on it, look at the
> -------middle finger so
> -------tall and straight,
> -------look at my pointer
> -------the most funniest
> -------finger. why? don't
> -------ask me, but I
> -------think it is the
> -------funniest. but

```
-------if all my fingers
-------work together
-------we'll have some-
-------thing swell, do you
-------know what?
-------we'll have,
-------guess—
a
whole
hand.
```
                    —*Richell Taylor, 7th*

Original visual form puts words in a perspective, out of their routine ap-pearances, forcing a fresh look at them. Jazzy line-breaks help light up the detailed mundanity.

"REAL-LIFE" PIECES

dark huge curled Indians Johnny Trojan
wolf beginning blueberries stream
drink owl branches climb shot
either rock.
                    —*Maribel, 4th*

This came from an exhortation to bring out in writing the details of minute-to-minute life, and I suppose she (rightly) felt her mind was a real place and went in there (mind as repository not directive machine). Stream-of-consciousness re-invented.

One day I lost my grandmother's change from going to the store. I was so scared I thought my hair would jump up and my clothing would jump off and while I was imagining all of that she walked in from work and she didn't feel good. And she said, where is my change? And I was stalling and, well, your penny was copper and your quarter was silver and your dollar was green. And she said, I know that and my coat is blue. And I started to laugh. And, all jokes aside, she said, where's my change? And I looked in my back pocket and I found it. Ha Ha Ha!
                    —*Chandra Brown, 4th*

Spirit lively via the use of everyday speech. Quickness of image and narrative.

One night I was lying down in my bed thinking if stars could fall like beautiful snowflakes. Like birds swooping down for fun. Like rain falling down very quietly. Like a feather floating down into your hands. That dream was so beautiful that in my sleep I put my head up and let it float down.
                    —*Shaneem, 3rd*

Bad grammar (as in "if" in the first line) may crack open a phrase and let out the unexpected. "If" leads on more than either/or "whether" would, moves us almost causally into the other movements, which are all different but all soft. Then, supposedly *out* of the dream, the physical head is still half in fantasy, floating down, transcending the facts of human body (neck).

> It was Friday in the night; there was a terrible sight. When I saw a very sad moment. Everyone was solid, like stone. Shaking there was, in everyone's bone. Sobbing and shivering in everybody's fear. Everywhere I looked I saw someone. Near. The granddaughter was watching it go away. She wanted it to stay but it couldn't. There was a sudden strike that, there was sympathy for a grandmother of four children and great-grandchild flowing away on a stretcher into a funeral car. Everyone was sad when they saw the beautiful grand.
> —*Angela Hill, 8th*

The unusual wording bespeaks concentration on the spirit of the moment (as opposed to narrative or descriptive logic), highlights the emotion, gets beyond cliché.

> The country is brave, bitter, and beautiful. Bears roam in the woods. Frogs splash in the pond. The horses cry in the rain. Birds sing night and day. Trees standing as high as mountains. Cows' voices bellowing in the wind. But it's still quiet. Too quiet.
> —*Terry, 5th*

The paradox of quiet and noise, spookiness arising with surprise yet appropriateness from a wilderness "painting" tinged with dream. The bears seem created from the four *b*'s in the first sentences. Then the repetition of consonants turns to the repetition of animals.

ABOUT POETRY

> Poetry is like words out of place.
> —*Shonell, 4th*

"Like" that, but not that.

> When I sit to write poetry I feel a very unusual person.
> When I can't think of something I look very fierce. I take glances, look at everything so I can get an idea.
> When I finish I feel temperamental.
> —*Danielle Lapointe, 5th*

Sincere exactitudes of the poetic process.

> Poems that I imagine in my mind are very dark and silly.
> Poems are like cold snow falling on the ground at night.
> Poems are like flags blue and white.
> The word "poem" is made up by a fat man.
> —*Yolanda Rowe, 4th*

"Dark and silly" is a wonderful slant combination. That is, upon reading "dark and" we expect, even in the instant before the next word comes, either a corollary (such as "gloomy") or an opposite (such as "light"). "Silly" contains tones of lightness but is far enough away to surprise as well. "Blue and white" and "fat man" seem so arbitrary as to be provocative.

> Poetry is something I can't understand. It's confusing too. I don't know what to say, but I like it. It's like going through a maze but not finding my way out....
>   I can't find my way out!
> I can't breathe! There are three doors. One leads to poetry, one leads to ice-skating, one leads to horse-riding. I open the door and out comes poetry. Oh how I love poetry!
>   —Millie Hernandez, 5th

The mystery and the choice of poetry clearly concretized as a story.

> Poems are so classy.
> They answer you right back.
>   —Tania Trovato, 4th

Surprise logic of street-talk.

> Poetry is like riding your new bike. Sometime you will like to get off your bike and sing your heart out and you may break a window but you tried your best and that is what you can do.
>   —Arita Charles, 4th

Lovely sincere rush at the end. Interesting that you have to get *off* the vehicle, like Wordsworth's explanation of poetry as emotion "recollected in tranquility."

> Poems are wild and deadly. When you are writing one it feels ike a monster is going to get you. You write and write till you're finished. The clouds are turning like you. Your poem is turning green and your heart is turning black till the poem is finished. The end of the poem and the end of you.
>   —Samantha Narcisse, 5th

How the poem spreads out and "turns" the whole scene, from clouds to heart.

The following five poems all derive a lot of their distinction from oddities of language. In each case the oddity seems chosen not out of facetiousness but out of a desire to express something for which no readymade vocabulary was available.

> Poetry is bright as sprinkles on top of three stars.
> We stand upon green a blue stars.
> I see Mrs. Borden singing to the green sprinkly stars.
> Like green pearls upon my blue eyes.
>   —Olga Rivera, 4th

Here the attempt is clearly to express a sense of beauty. The originality of the vision has made it hard for Olga to resolve, but its strength, especially in the last line, tends to offset its confusion.

> Poetry can swift you away
> like a balloon

> taking you on a trip
> to a wonderful
> place beyond your dreams.
> —*Bruce Johnson, 6th*

"Swift" as a verb vivifies an otherwise ordinary image.

> Writing a poem is like eating a harsh brain.
> Writing a poem is like eating dirt if you ate it before.
> —*Monique Allen, 4th*

"Harsh brain" by itself is more potent an eating image than Stephen Crane's bitter heart. Line 2 by association makes the brain earthier yet.

> When I do poems it is silly to know
> what to do.
> Bees fly near me.
> Yes they do.
> And the horse
> kicks me home.
> Instead of doing my homework
> I do poetry.
> —*Mildred Matos, 4th*

"Silly to know what to do" expresses the certainty in imagination. The "yes they do" bees and kicking horse combine nature's dangers with honey and home. Last two lines are weak.

> Poem is nice, it goes
> under my legs and it
> comes right back to
> my head, it goes around
> and around and stops,
> and goes to my body
> and doesn't stop.
> —*Sammy Ramos, 5th*

With a shaky command of English, this student manages to convey a sense that poetry remains active in the body whereas in the head alone (intellect) it becomes repetitive and stops.

> My hand is out of energy.
> My mind is up in the sky.
> When I write I do mistakes and poetry passes my mind and
> my head is lost.
> And birds over my mind.
> —*Jose C., 3rd*

Sincere yet visual. Dissociation of poem and self at least results in "birds," which may come down to earth further along. It's a nice surprise that the figurative "up in the sky" becomes literal (in the "birds") two lines later.

The power of innocence shines strongly in the wording of this poem. When

Jose's a little older he may not be able to talk (or think) like this. I can only hope he finds in his grown-up world ways to speak that are as calm, exact, and personal as "my hand is out of energy."

Chapter VII

ENERGY

"Poetry is like a basketball bouncing in my head"

Energy can be considered the basic quality everywhere, but in this chapter's poems energy is not only basic but paramount. In some cases such energy works by exemplification: the very abundance of words, an on-going rhythm, "wildness" of images, and a sense of "Brownian movement" in the changes rung within the poem. In some cases the poems may seem excessive. Kids often have difficulty finding acceptable vehicles for the release of their imaginative energy and it builds up. When poetry then provides an outlet the release can be quite powerful or "too much" or both. Even when it's too much, an abundance of energy in words is always promising.

Another way energy can be emphasized is simply by being spoken of. When a child writes as if everything, even inanimate objects, were alive, the feeling is of a world of energy, stones still crackling with the fires that formed them, walls living in human-like relationships. While candidness, the leading quality discussed in the previous chapter, may also produce a "wild" image or a series of unexpected changes, it seems a relatively contemplative state. When candor gathers momentum and goes from a walk to a run, I have called it energy.

ACROSTICS

When I woke up I found a rat that
Is not a rat, it's Superman. Not bad, it's not Superman.
Loco loco diablo. Is that—no, it's not loco loco diablo, It's—
Look, just tell me the truth!
I'm not one of you, so shut up.
Ay, Tell me the truth.
My name is Monkey-sees-monkey-does.
Oh, now I know you, you
Rooster, you are Monkey-sees-monkey-does.

Take this. That? This, this!
I'm not for that, I'm for some
Zebras. They are black and brown.
    —*William Ortiz, 3rd*

His own name, of course, contains anything at all. Scattershot infusion of energy into any old thing, no qualifications. The instant-to-instant mind, like a wind tunnel of verbal sparks.

Why are walls
All the same? Because they're
Like twins
Living in the
Same room.
    —*Linda Nicole, 5th*

Anthropomorphic animism. At least a perception of "life" in an unlikely place, the inscrutable wall.

F is my favorite
Letter. My name is
O-face. I like
Wabbits. I eat roaches and
Easy
Relatives. I eat rats too. *And* snakes.
    —*David Vigo, 1st*

A wildflower.

Tania is me. Some people call me E.T. I hate them. I call them a
    little donkey.
Alice is my cousin. She is very nice to me. I love her as she
    likes me.
Nephews are nice to have they are small. But mine is not small
    at all.
Irish people are rich. So am I.
And a tramp goes along the street, screaming up and down.
    —*Tania, 3rd*

"Little donkey," "love her as she likes me," "but mine is not small at all," the whole of line 4, and the extravagant lilt of line 5 add up to a charming montage. Each line has a special charm and they accelerate.

LUNE (EXTENDED)

It is dawn,
as beautiful as Goldie Hawn.
The planes fly
deep in the sky, high,
while poor birds

fall off a roof and
land flat dead.
Deep in the clouds children
go to bed,
and a big blue bird
up in heaven.
TWA just turned eleven.
        —*Anthony Fraticelli, 5th*

One of the many occasions the extended lune (continuing the alternation of three- and five-word lines) has been invented. This one rambles and rhymes with good humor.

THING POEM

NYC STREET

Car honking people talking all the stores open big crowds in the stores drop your 20-dollar package does anybody care no nobody they all just step on it they don't look where they're going just want to get home!
        —*Juan Martinez, 7th*

The poignance of "does anybody care no nobody" stands out in this setting. Lack of punctuation is appropriate for the street stream. The speed doesn't miss a beat into genuine speech.

WILLIAM CARLOS WILLIAMS IMITATIONS

Sis, I am very sorry for spoiling
your date last night by pouring juice
on your white dress, pulling off your
wig, cutting your boyfriend's hair,
eating up the whole pizza, refusing
to give you the umbrella when it
started to rain and for pouring
water on your head so your mascara
ran and you looked like a raccoon,
but I had loads of *fun*!
        —*Evanne Keith, 4th*

Wild expansion of the swiped-plums ideas in the Williams original.

So much depends upon
an acrostic for poetry
an elephant
a zoo
a universe

a solar system
the world
a sun
a moon
some stars
an orbit for the earth
a reservoir
land
water
schools
classes
teachers
poems
sonnets
math
poetry
good grades
vocabulary
homework
reading
story-telling contests
talent shows
spelling
people
numbers
the alphabet
trees
animals
forests
rain
paper
faces
bodies
hospitals
doctors
nurses
babies
food
            —*Robert Brown, 2nd*

Wild expansion of a red wheelbarrow.

VARIOUS POEMS

a kid as you know
sometimes right, sometimes wrong.
I ask what is fair, I've never
found it, probably never will.

you get pushed from all ways around
you. you look as if you see a giant ready
to step on you. you hardly can't chew
because they're stuffed with worries and hurt.
you fight and you still get stomped on
    by the killer.
you try to say what you feel and want. but then
the evil takes over. when you sorrow people
laugh you try your best to make them
feel pity unwanted, scared to live
like a beaten puppy with skin hurdled up
his back like if he was burned from
    the witch above,
laughing like a crackling man pounding
    out of his grave
with misery and spooks eating his flesh with disgust.
I'm a champion in my ways
that no one else can understand. it's like
    a needle

going in my arm and the evil commands it
    to retreat
and go back in its life and rot away.
when I do my work the evil makes me shake
and makes me do wrong and write funny like now.
it's taking charge of my willpower and guts to
stand up for what I think and feel.
I write what I feel and never stop
but I have to go, midnight evil is dragging
me back to the hole of terror too shocking
to say! worms fill my eyes and bats eat my
toes my body is attacked by killer whales.
my mind is not attacked by any human animal or
anything will enter sub-zero experience! and
the most horrible duel man has
received yet and won't be the last or even
unwording to the highest and mightiest thing
that I shall punish and put a stop to! or I'm
not what I yam!
    —Aaron, 7th

This too is a wild expansion, perhaps of the Pandora's Box inside everyone. Poetically, this is a great disturb-o-spill, but in writing terms as well as human terms the piece does cry out for selective control and some focus away from the intense subjectivity. Along the way, a number of felicitous usages occur, such as "skin hurdled up," "pounding out of his grave," and "sub-zero experience." I don't think a poem like this should be criticized for its emotional content—better the violence be composed on paper than anywhere else—but for its confusion of movement, repetition, derivativeness. Praise is due the obvious talent and effort. "If you're angry, write it out, but do a good job."

Gently, the student could be led to write (for practice, for fun) about things to which the anger simply doesn't apply, though a lack of interest in anything outside the head-world of rage may be hard to get through. Such children often have strong verbal gifts, and wordplay may help lead the writing out of self-obsession.

> caged like a beast hanged
> from his ears tossed in the
> terror room, get chopped up
> then grinded up, blended
> with sour milk!
> disgusting? wisely true
> then pouring in the mouth
> of the be trader torn flesh
> fed to the one of the wise
> then the ignorant get a double
> scooper of mellow ice cream
> be treated like kings, yuk!
> if that was me I'd be fed to the dogs
> my remains eaten by pickles and
> eyes rolling on your salad, big man.
> then spit on you
> you get nauseous
> uptight and try to
> do back and almost
> regret your life.
> —Aaron, 7th

From the same poet, though for a different assignment ("real-life" writings). New words, same subjective focus, violence and paranoia. Same sense of talent beyond the pale.

ABOUT POETRY

> I think of poetry like it is backwards, poem a writing about poem a writing instead of writing a poem about writing a poem. Poetry is like a million words because you use them. Poetry is like a plant, a plant grows then it dies just like your mind is thinking good but goes away. Poetry is like a car it goes somewhere then it comes back. Poetry is like the two flags, the first one has 13 stars just like your mind is 13% and the second has 50 stars like your mind has 50% but better. Poetry is like Christopher Columbus when he discovered America just like you made up the words "Christopher Columbus discovered America." The End.
> —Gino Chiusano, 4th

Again, the scattered richnesses of disturbance. The last sentence is a keen disclosure of levels of poetic discovery.

Poetry is like a basketball bouncing in my head and it flies out of
my ear and I take a shot and the backboard yells POETRY and I
say Shut up back to the backboard and the shot goes in and the
backboard falls on top of me.
　　　—*Kevin Kay, 4th*

The struggle and speeds of mind shown concretely, in regard to composition
and its excited ups and downs. The role of the backboard is interesting; it is
simultaneously restrictive and helpful.

Poetry takes you places. It takes you to Japan, the future, the
sky, the sun. Sometimes it takes you places you don't want to go.
It could be a bother or a sport. You don't have to take a car or a
bus. You take your mind. You don't have to pack clothing. You
pack words. *&* to Japan we go.
　　　—*Enioca Joseph, 5th*

Japan/future/sky/sun—a progression in types of destination, each move a surprise. Bother vs. sport—a slant opposition, more interesting than the simplicity of directness. Ideas then fill out gracefully in what "you" have to take and
pack. This rhythm leads to the last sentence, the lyric lift of immediate speech,
"*&* to Japan we go."

Chapter VIII

SURPRISE

"A beautiful ballerina twirling/ around the block"

The tones of surprise may be seen as forming a spectrum of emotions. The various lights of context may allow areas of this spectrum to show themselves as humor or poetry — or both — or just plain shock.

All humor is based on incongruity. Given one thing, we expect to find another in conjunction with it. This is a simple way of stating the intelligibility of life on earth. When the incongruous occurs we may feel horror, or bewilderment, or joy, but the possibility of humor is always there. In a poem, expectations arise either through the use of known forms or through setting up a certain rhythm of events. Then they're either fulfilled or to some degree violated. If no significant violations of expectation occur, a work or passage may still be humorous by that very extreme. That is, we are accustomed to some surprise coming in all things.

In poetry the condensation, emphasis on measure and sound correspondences, and lack of dependence on linear thought move the sources of incongruity more clearly into the physical aspects of language.

The old meaning of "humor(s)" is quite different from, but related to, today's. The word comes from the Latin for moisture or fluid and centuries ago referred in English to the body fluids (blood, phlegm, and yellow and black bile) considered responsible for one's health and disposition. From this the meaning of the word shifted to mood, then fancy or caprice and thus to comicality. Having a physical base and historic identities with one's entire disposition and fancies, it's no wonder that humor is a strong element in poetry. It's not just jokes, escapism. With the phenomenological gap between perception and "objective reality" setting up continual incongruities everywhere we look, it can be said that humor, serious or light, is a prime ingredient of poetry.

Ambivalence, or ambiguity, is a strong element in humor as well as in poetry. Ambivalence is, in a sense, surprise fanned out into a cluster of understandings, the shock diffused, even subtlized, into possibilities.

Some of the poems in this chapter lead up to one big surprise at the end. Some even have a double surprise as climax. In others the continuing quality of the language, when word-to-word choices are being made rather than formulae followed, may contain surprise as a recurrent, or at least occasional, characteristic. These syntactical surprises draw attention to points that may be parts of the poet's intention (as in the "INCREDIBLE" acrostic below) or may open up serendipitous side-issues, many of which turn out to connect meaningfully within the poems.

Of course, surprise is the fruit of everything the poem has: tone, soundplay, and rhythm as well as ladders and twists of meaning.

The physical shapes and motions in a poem may create a setting in which the thought can shine, touch, or proliferate (as in the "CROSS" acrostic below).

When surprise occurs in a poem, it tends to validate the surrounding or previous material. This may not be so if the surprise is *just* a joke or results in a very limited surface understanding, or is so blatant as to blunt the tone and block out any subtlety. But when the surprise has implications, connotations (as in the last line of the "floor" poem on p. 73) that spread out more or less endlessly (ambivalence), the other parts of the poem are thereby deepened, especially if they are rather "open" in meaning and seem at first to be simply descriptive. This sort of openness is common in children's poems.

Surprise is definitely a manifestation of energy. And surprise is candid. What separates these poems from those in the previous two chapters is, again, emphasis rather than some fundamental difference. When the essence of the poem seems to me to lie in the way one or more phrases are "set up" to stand out, like secular epiphanies, I've classed it here: jack-in-the-box words and tone changes.

If a poem is very short, the whole thing can be a gulp of surprise.

ACROSTICS

Embarking on the
Never-ending flight of the
Dark world they call
Love,
Expect to receive
Something
Spectacular, and you get dumped.
—*Roseanne Cordero, 8th*

The obvious shock of "and you get dumped," plays against the fancy tone of the preliminary language, as well as against its meaning and the backbone word "ENDLESS." The surprise *is* a bit heavy-handed. Nice variety of rhythm and line-length.

Inside of everybody everything can be.
Nice, for God gives you a brain.

Can you think of a way that you can
Read a great saying and say,
"Everybody, let's sing a song in harmony."
Did you ever have something incredible
In your own home?
Be a winner.
Let's all be incredible!
Everybody, come on!
—*Daniel Nurimow, 3rd*

Each sentence contains some oddity of speech that advances the point, that life can be *incredible*.

Winter is a bad bunch of days.
I hate winter.
Nothing keeps you warm.
Things like food get cold fast.
End, winter, end.
Roll away.
—*Sojourna Thompson, 5th*

The rhythm of each sentence lying within one line helps, in this case, to main-tain a curt, grumpy tone. "End, winter, end" would be a fair end but merely leads up, as it turns out, to the beautiful "Roll away," its brevity packing power, its instant visual impact and fantastic nature acting in contrast to the mundanity and generality of the other lines.

Love is like a dove flying
Over the ocean in a flash
Very late in the
Evening, saying, "How about a date?"
—*Venus Rhodes, 6th*

Sudden blatant contrast in both logos and melos, thought and sound. The two parts combine to expose effectively the quick foolishness of love.

Climbing a mountain and
Reaching the top seems to
Open the gates of the
Sun rising and
Shining over me.
—*Joyce Walters, 5th*

The relationship of "CROSS" to the lines is original but immediately clear, religious spirit calling out the light. Three-D effect. One ascension "opens the gates" for another. The vertical "CROSS" intersects with the horizontally ex-pansive view and light. The openness of the line endings helps the openness of the thought and the geometry. "Me" is a conclusive conclusion.

Mysterious and
Young,
Sometimes not

Enough to
Let myself
Flow through.
    —Anonymous, 6th

The ambivalence here is hard to grasp but it works in terms of the subject—the confusions of the self. I guess the "wholeness" of the infant—mysterious and young enough to let the self flow through—is a fair take.

Brown is a color that I happen to
Like
Under the
Earth all day and night.
    —Juemell Ballou, 6th

Kind of an unexpected burial. "Happen" helps it just lie there, in the interesting condition of light or no light, there where the sun doesn't shine. Makes us think about the color existing without light. "BLUE" is the opposite of brown in this layout, sky vs. earth, though not scientifically. The blue, as spine word, is implicit in the "brown" talk, as perhaps the sky is implicit by opposition when we talk particularly of earth.

Though my
Heart
Is breaking,
Still I like to dance.
    —Vicki Babb, 4th

This is it. One can picture the brave dance, jiggling the cracked heart dangerously but nobly. "Like to" is unpretentious, keeps it from being "too much," in the way that "Still I wipe my tears and dance" would be.

Blue is a color, a
Lovely color that is
Under the sun
Everywhere, even in thunder.
    —Stacy, 1st

Repetition of "color" works well with the doubling in the last line, especially with the two "ev's," and with the thunder/under sound. "Under the sun" a pretty line—blue seems ultimately high to us, but it's under the sun, whose rays catalyze it. Synesthesia at the end (color in sound, in this case) doubles things again.

Madness is terrible. It is
A horrible thing.
Don't you just love it?
    —Marilyn Gonzales, 6th

Mom
And
Dad
    —Anonymous, 9th

Two good jokes, turning clearly on surprise, the second so short that the whole of it is a quick surprise.

> Night stays in a can like soda
> Until someone opens it.
> Then it fizzes,
> Squirting all over your face.
> —*Lamar Gardner, 5th*

Crazy darkness. The strain of picturing darkness so palpable goes well with the nutsy backbone word.

> Volcanoes erupting
> Ashes falling
> Lava everywhere
> Expecting my death
> Naturally I'm scared
> Tomorrow I'm dead...
> Inspiring horse comes galloping by
> Never have I jumped up so high
> Eternity is waiting for me, but they'll have to wait.
> —*Veronica Fernandez, 5th*

Love ("VALENTINE") is survival. "Inspiring" is a neat word. It takes a deep breath and high jump to get on top of it. The ambiguous "they" in Eternity is a delight.

> Water
> All over me.
> Light shining at me.
> Life around me.
> —*Johnsuat Padua, 4th*

The contrast between the limits of "wall" and the limitlessness of water, light, and life, and the way "wall" is vertical and the other words flow out horizontally make this poem a pictorial surprise.

PLACE POEMS

> My room's dark
> and cold. I close my
> eyes and dream of ghosts,
> and wake up with a white blanket.
> —*Miguel Oliveras, 7th*

Dream and reality overlap at the point of awakening. The palpable ghost (blanket) seems benevolent, and seems not to have been there when sleep began!

> My room is fun because I can listen to my records and I can mess up
> my room and I can invite my friends. When I am alone in my room

> I love to jump on my bed and dance and when I am with my sister I
> love to do the moon walk. Sometimes I am scared of my room.
> —*Lillian Lopez, 5th*

The fear that underlies the most mellow situation comes as a shock, barely anticipated by "moon."

LUNES

> Black is black,
> white is white. Then what
> is bright yellow?
> —*Carlos A., 4th*

The ambivalence of color is concisely shown. Extremes (black and white) are extremes, flat. The "bright" both emphasizes and brings out a new expression of the yellow as opposed to either of the colorless opposites. It's more than the word "yellow," as a flat term, is.

> Think of me
> as a beautiful ballerina twirling
> around the block.
> —*Shirley Marc, 5th*

The first line is low-key, sets up the next line, which is extravagant when you look (listen) closely. The rhythm is fancy (da-da-DA-da-da DA-da-DA-da DA-da), dances nicely with the alliteration of b's, r's, and l's and with the vowel-play, especially the a's. It amounts to an early climax to the poem. The participle keeps the movement alive, unresolved, at line's end, like a ballerina *en pointe*. Then the last line, a cunning anticlimax, brings the glory of that picture down to a situation so ordinary and local its reduction is quite poignant (but she's still dancing!)

> I wake up.
> I see the sun. I
> have to eat.
> —*Andrew Ariana, 3rd*

The extreme simplicity makes the reader wonder whether Andrew has to eat for hunger's sake or because he's called. Is the sight of the sun appetizing or a reminder of time? Either way, a sudden reduction in scope energizes the poem. The vowels show a nice, lively alternation of dull and sharp tones.

> The purple flower
> on the green grasses, so
> I sit down.
> —*Dominick Gallusso, 3rd*

The nifty progression occurs doubly, when the "so" (then reinforced by the sentence-fragment nature of the whole poem) suddenly interposes a colloquial tone into the romantic nature mood, and then the perfect precipitation from such a combination, the brass-tacks, present-tense "I sit down." The curt sound of the last four words helps clinch the move.

> You know what
> I mean when I say
> I love you.
> —*Evelyn Bourdier, 8th*

The vowels form a parabola cresting at "mean," so the sly joke gently wins true, that is, the emphasis on "mean" underscores the love's questionability. At the same time, the poem is all monosyllables, with no tricky consonant combinations, so the sound slips by quickly. The flow of the vowels dominates. The "I love you" is past us before we catch the connotation, makes us do a double-take.

> The sun is
> nice as a blue jay singing
> away to Hollywood.
> —*Edith Orsini, 5th*

A little exuberance. The singing blue jay is odd as a comparison for the sun but catches the positive spirit. Then the playfulness is upped another notch in the third line, not only by "Hollywood" but also by the unusual use of "away to." Note how the galloping rhythm helps the tone.

> When my aunt
> starts cooking dinner, *everybody* says
> see you later.
> —*Anonymous, 6th*

and

> When I talk
> I can't stop at all
> you know me.
> —*Cassandra Moore, 7th*

Obvious kicker in last line of each, with sudden speed, but each depends on perfect rhythm lead-up, mostly the vivaciousness of everyday speech.

> rock shock the
> house. everybody to the funky
> beat. yes yes.

●

> I like bacon,
> toast, eggs, milk, orange-juice and
> very cold water.
> —*Juemell Ballou, 5th*

These two were written by the same girl in ten minutes, showing dramatically the range of tones possible in a little poem, or two, when the focus is on language.

> When I see
> that you are being nice,
> watch what happens.
> —*Monifa Reel, 5th*

I've asked classes which way they feel the meaning goes ("I" respond happily to "your" niceness, or "your" niceness may conceal an evil intent?), and opinion has been evenly divided. The measured rhythm, the word "watch," and the way line 3 is set off in the imperative may carry an ominous tone. A strongly balanced and witty ambivalence.

> She was a
> very stupid lady, but she
> got over it.
> —*Preya Singh, 5th*

A very funny, also serious, thought, economically put, with the surprise packed in the last line.

> Black black black
> is an interesting color but
> what a sound.
> —*Jeanette Orsini, 5th*

First the sound is emphasized by the triple mention, then the color is spoken of, then the sound. The quick flow through "is" and "but" makes sight and sound almost simultaneous.

> Paint me up.
> Paint me all around town.
> Paint me down.
> —*Rhonda Coleman, 1st*

Try to picture this and find exact meaning—you can't. That resistance is lyric substance.

> Three men are
> looking up to the sky,
> high high high.
> —*Robert Diaz, 1st*

Just a strange and lovely picture, one "high" for each man.

> Today is Friday.
> Thursday is before Friday and
> didn't you know.
> —*Lil Nicasio, 3rd*

Poker-faced simple-mindedness suddenly lit up in the last line.

> Books eat words
> and pictures eat colors up.

You do too.
            —*Jon Fong, 4th*

A nice concrete way to state the domination of wholeness, in artwork and, coming as a surprise, in people.

I remember when
I saw the clouds kiss
my dog today.
            —*Jose Rosario, 3rd*

The word "dog" is the epitome of an endearing, awkward earthiness, con-trasting with the worn-out loveliness of "clouds kiss."

The stars are
white, the sun is yellow.
I like it.
            —*Omar Lama, 4th*

Sudden tone shift with last line. Retroactive ambivalence of just what is liked, whether sun or situation. The odd distinction between white and yellow here is charming, though scientifically off.

When the President
dies he turns to sand
just like me.
            —*Paul Olivarria, 5th*

Sudden voice change for last line; an image of dignity and pity.

THING POEMS

The hand is like a mind of its own.
The fingers are like God with his angels.
Your hand is like Jesus wisdom but
If you don't be careful you might
End up one hand short.
            —*Edward Peterson, 6th*

To say "is like" in line 1 instead of "has" is, as it were, a mistake, but results in a more interesting concept, the feeling that mind and physicality interpene-trate thoroughly (kept up later with the "Jesus wisdom" line). Bold angel image-ry in the middle, and then the ending brings the metaphysics down to earth.

Floor,
How are you?
Are you blue?
I don't think so.
Does it hurt when someone bounces the ball?
I feel sorry when they step on you.
Does it hurt when they step on you?

Doesn't it bother you if you're dirty?
How old are you? Are you thirsty?
Do you get mad
Or do you get glad?
Do you have eyes?
Do you cry?
Do you go to sleep?
Are you very deep?
    —*Mayra Reyes, 6th*

A balance of in-and-out rhyme. Progression of "soulfulness" in the questions
(but not programmatic). Good last line helps every previous line.

The city streets are funny and fun. When summer comes we can
open the pump in our block and go into the water and go to Central Park to their swimming pool, and the winter is funny and
fun. You can go sledding, hit people with white fluffy snowballs
and watch people fall on their behinds yah.
    —*Anonymous, 5th*

The charm here is in the nice but not striking summer/winter fun portrayal
setting up the sudden barbaric yawp "yah."

A nose is like a hole in the wall.
But that's not all. It falls between
your mouth and your eyes, but when it
falls it snores.
    —*Jose Rodriguez, 7th*

"But that's not all" is quietly crazy-funny following the particular oddness of
the first image. Economy of the move between the two kinds of "fall." Then, in
the last line, the humor changes suddenly from the charms of syntax to a
deliberate joke, snappily done.

WILLIAM CARLOS WILLIAMS IMITATION

I'm sorry that I ate your lunch.
I'm sorry that I ate your breakfast.
I'm sorry that I'm going to eat your supper.
    —*Carlos Cintron, 4th*

The time-turnaround of the first two lines helps keep the emphasis away from
a simple rush and lets the reader's attention concentrate on the ruthless,
taciturn surprise of "going to."

VARIOUS POEMS

The good side of love is meeting
someone that cares about you.

But the bad side of love is
when that certain person who cares
about you falls for another girl.
Then you slap him in the face.
That's another good side of love.
        —*Virginia A., 6th*

At first I thought the words "certain," "who cares," and "about you" should be eliminated, but I see them now as building up an atmospheric contrast for the action/concept double punchline.

The rose began to open and I saw it
I like to see a rose open, it is like wilderness
wilderness is like a rose
like a rose is wilderness
        —*Mildred Luciano, 5th*

"Wilderness" a "wow" word as it comes in, and then the last two lines make a fine distinction within that lovely coupling of small and vast ("is like" reaching in and "is" reaching out), i.e., something is like its part but the part *is* the whole— contrary to "fact" but true to a certain spirit, and to an emphasis on spirit.

The sun is clear but never near.
When does it come out?
One at a time.
        —*John Chang, 4th*

"Clear...never near" locates the sun, for us, at the crossing point of two different prime facts of it. Mysterious, "Zen" quality of last two lines, compounding time and space and hinting that each new day brings a different sun. On top of all this, the poem is an acrostic of "two."

I was watching the sun rise
and the sun rose very pretty.
My brother came and watched the sun
rise too. My little brother was
looking at a picture of the stars,
then he looked outside and was
looking for stars, and I said
that the stars don't come out
in the morning. He said, stars
are very pretty and I said, I
like stars too.
        —*Julia Papleo, 6th*

Touching switch from an information base to emotion.

I was sitting down in my living room, watching TV alone. I wanted to open the window because it was hot as hell. As I opened it I saw a man in a dark suit on a motorcycle driving very fast to try to pass the red light in the street. Another car was passing through there, and the motorcycle crashed into the car and

the man flipped over the car. I couldn't believe it, so I closed the window and went back to watching TV. But I couldn't stop thinking about it and thought, "Maybe it really happened."
—*Anonymous, 7th*

Real/unreal, involving the ambivalence of television and also that of "hell."

"REAL-LIFE" PIECES

THE DARK

It was dark,
the stars were out,
and the moon too.
There was a house on the
corner, rocks on the ground,
the distant cry of a cricket.
I love TV.
—*Anonymous, 9th*

Wild surprise, extreme without seeming arbitrary. Several ideas make themselves felt: that conventional beauty is dull, that the nature images are meaningfully distilled only *on* TV, that nature is scary, that TV and poetry or speech similarly distort (so why not watch TV?), that distortion is O.K. "Rocks on the ground" makes for a primitive sense that increases the last line's power.

Crash of thunder,
flash of lightning,
a summer rain.
See the people run,
tall ones, short ones,
fat ones, thin ones,
old ones, young ones,
black and white.
And me with my
blue jeans and motorcycle.
—*Phillip Soto, 5th*

The day I was walking down the street,
me and my friend,
with red sweatshirts, blue jeans and
puffed vests.
We saw my boyfriend and his friend.
My boyfriend had on a cutoff gray sweatshirt
and green slacks.
His friend had on a blue mock neck and jeans with
green feet on the back pocket.
We smiled.
They smiled.
My boyfriend said, "I have to quit you."

I fainted.
When I came around I cried like a seagull in pain.
        —*Denise Smith, 6th*

One Friday my friend and I had the best time. We listened to a
wild rock group nearly blowing our ears off. After a while I
asked her to spend the night at my house. "I have to go home and
get my clothes." So we went to her house; we rode the broken-
down elevator down to the first floor. While we were walking
we saw a dalmatian with a polka-dot fur cover; he was barking
wildly. We went to her house; it was a big old building. Then
back we went to my house with our blue jeans and pink Jordache
shirts. We were so happy we sprang up from the ground like
springs in an old couch.
        —*Cassandra Roper, 6th*

Three strong surprises. A spot of color in a pencil sketch (Phillip's). Extreme use
of detail base to prepare lyric shot (Denise's). And in Cassandra's the sudden
motion (springing) of the happiness is (only then) immediately seen as inevitable.

ABOUT POETRY

Poetry is like the sun in my face.
I don't let it trouble my brain,
and like the cloud blocking the sun.
It's night now, the moon is coming out
as white as paper.
        —*Omar, 4th*

Being like both the sun *and* its concealment well represents the form/content
fight/ commingling of poetry. Line 2 sets up the quiet shock of the moon's ir-
resistible scribble-on-me call. It may not trouble your brain but it keeps coming
back, through blockage and darkness.

Poetry is like a sky scraping the skyscraper.
        —*Anthony, 4th*

Take that! The underdog has its day. But "sky" is not, on closer examination,
your typical underdog. Poetry is made to seem all-encompassing and, when its
softness is taken advantage of, a little feisty.

A poem is like
electricity blowing
through a telephone. I
answer if it sounds
like somebody is in trouble
but at the same time
laughing.
        —*Bernardo Aybar, 7th*

Lines 2 and 3 powerfully express energy forced through matter. Trouble and laughter form a prime diameter of poetry. The humor, a parody of sensitivity, is in being able to hear that oddly mixed tone in the ring itself.

Many of the poems in this chapter involve the reader in a sudden alteration of perspective. These rapid changes may be between reality and appearance, large and small, love and its lack, fact and quality, talking and crying out, sound and sight, sense and nonsense, rhythm and image, inside and out, and so forth. Involved readers get a sudden shock, and also a perspective on perspectives; they can derive from these poems and their energetic transitions a sense of the utter richness of the myriads of possible viewpoints available and, as a corollary, the limits of any one. Writers of course learn likewise as they make the poems.

Chapter IX

RHYTHM, RHYME, AND OTHER SOUNDS

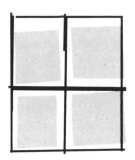

"Even in a turtle/ notion you can find a fish's swimming motion"

At the beginning of many residencies, while saying a few introductory words about poetry, or while speaking of the first poem or two read aloud to the class, whenever the word "rhythm" is evoked, I do a little demonstration I consider valuable. I tell them *anything* we say (beyond one syllable) has rhythm. Many are incredulous. Though they instinctively "know" their speech is loaded with rhythm—they demonstrate this by the choices they make every second they talk—they don't have it in mind. So I walk around the room and pick something unlikely (unlikely in that the *meaning* is so unromantic as to preclude a thought of rhythm—we are so fooled by associations), like "Please tell your parents to attend the September P.T.A. meeting." I read this off and ask if it has rhythm. Most say no. Then I repeat it a number of times, not exaggerating but letting the natural rhythm of it come to the fore, perhaps "paraphrase" it into "doo-da" syllables. Everybody sees (hears) the rhythm (and the *p* and *t* percussion), and presumably turns that insight in on their own speech.

Children tend to have a very clear rhythm in their regular talk—a sort of fortuitous combination of innocence and experience. They've spent thousands and thousands of hours speaking and listening, have the expertise of practice, but they're less likely than adults to feel they have to force their speech into acceptable patterns, abstraction, or tones of colorless dignity. The strong, basic Anglo-Saxon rhythms emerge more in the speech of children (and working-class adults) than in that of the intellectually educated, to whom rhythmic speech may seem (consciously or not) crude, a diversion from intelligence. But, poetically, rhythm punches or touches ideas home.

Some people mistakenly think that mastery of rhythm in poetry consists in being able to cast one's language into a regular beat. Even in the heyday of meter, such a skill was only the beginning. Masters of rhythm such as Milton gained their distinction via the *variations* of rhythm they could introduce and still hew to the measure, and how appropriately expressive each variation was. Here are the first four lines of *Paradise Lost*:

> Of Man's first disobedience, and the fruit
> Of that forbidden tree, whose mortal taste
> Brought death into the world, and all our woe,
> With loss of Eden, till one greater Man

Read this aloud, using normal speech rhythms. Read it several times. No boomp-de-boomp boredom at all, yet it is perfect iambic pentameter (if I'm right in assuming "into" was meant to be accented lightly on its second syllable).

Some of the ways Milton achieves rhythmic variety are:

• Varying syllable length, especially such a diphthongy extension as "dience"

  • Secondary accents ("and" in line 1, "ience," and "to")
  • Caesura and its varied placement
  • Grammatical units continuing into the next line
  • Consonantal jam (such combinations as "nsf," "rstd," and "ndth," all in the first line). Note how "Brought death" is slowed by its own sound, especially *t* to *d* (breath to voice), and thereby draws attention.

Alliteration is woven contrapuntally throughout, and the vowel assortment is rich within each line.

Contrast Milton's sound with this line, also iambic pentameter: "The dog is running through the growing grass." Such a rhythm quickly becomes boring. The syllables here are about the same length. The only places two consonant sounds come together—*s/r, ng/thr,* and *ng/gr*—don't slow the tongue's movement. *Ng* and *th* constitute one phoneme each, and *r* is a semi-vowel. There is no clear caesura, and sentence corresponds with line. No secondary accents, partly due to a lack of more than two-syllable words.

It would take too long to speak here of the expressive qualities of Milton's music, how these rhythmic complexities work together with meaning and feeling.

In modern poetry, the outstanding rhythms tend to be free-form; not that they don't play off patterns, but they play further off them, as good jazz does. This is no less an achievement, more difficult in a way because it starts from scratch.

I don't advocate teaching kids Miltonic rhythm. I do frequently point out to them, in simple terms, such intricacies as are in this lune by a Nebraska high school student.

> A raindrop falls.
> It falls on my nose.
> Delicate, light, transparent.

The second line is almost without rhythm. The monosyllables are nearly equally weighted, as speech goes. Then the third line (transcending its shorter word-count) bursts out into an elegant, fancy rhythm, the commas dividing it to dactyl, accented syllable, amphibrach. The shift is perfectly expressive, from the mundanity in monorhythm of a drop on the nose (which protuberance often leads to comedy) to the sober ecstasy of the last line, as if we are sudden-ly looking through a microscope.

The best way to bring kids to an awareness of rhythm is to start with what they've got—not only the complex rhythms of everyday talk but also such ac-tivities as having a heartbeat, walking, skipping, broken-field running, Double Dutch, and doing the Moonwalk.

Being less set in their verbal structures, children are more likely than adults to come up with new, spontaneous snatches of mouth-music. This sort of thing is a famous delight ("Kids say the darndest things," "Hey, guess what my daughter said yesterday"), but we don't take the instances seriously, or follow the implications.

Of course good grown-up poets do carry poetic sound to sustained glories of which children are incapable. I am not suggesting that Percy Nunez exceeds Pope or Milton, or Charles Olson or Frank O'Hara. However, I readily suggest he exceeds (in the "OCEAN" acrostic below), even in sophistication, the vivacity and mastery of sound (including sound's relations to meaning) shown by the majority of adult published poets, especially those who try, without a lifetime of intense assimilation, to fit their work into solemn metrical and rhyme schemes, and also those who abjure any quality of song in favor of dwelling on "psychological" values.

Repetition is an extreme form of rhythm, as rhyme and its variants (asso-nance, alliteration) are, in part, rhythm devices. Teachers should not, for vari-ety's sake, make repetition a no-no. Repetition can enchant, like a drug, until altogether new senses of word or phrase break into mind (as staring at any lit-tle thing a long time will cause it to "change"). Repetition can focus one's at-tention on tiny variations. It can set things up for the power of a big change.

List poems are condensed, as poetry is "supposed" to be. They break up or eliminate extraneous thought bridges and overlays and may simulate actual mental process, leaping from thing to thing. They may clarify relationships be-tween things via the method's non-interference, juxtapositional nakedness. They're natural fields for strong rhythm. The form encourages "random" pro-gressions transcending the errors and limits of conscious thought.

When I ask the average class, at first, to tell me something about poetry, chances are the first response is "It rhymes." In large part this view is a regret-table diminution of poetry, often reflecting the cheapest uses of it. But children love rhyme. Adults love rhyme. Many in the poetry workshop business have scorned rhyme because we know more subtly expressive alternatives, and because we know kids do abuse rhyme, let it take over and thus blot out everything else (and because we've been following our own historic rebellion). But rhyme is great; it does give a simple power, often funny by the nature of sound (extreme emphases). It makes solid connections. Also, kids often use rhyme in scattered ways, thus not committing the inaccuracy of over-regularizing life's energies. As with rhythm, the technique of rhyme is misunderstood. To find rhymes and still be able to say something is only the beginning. Skilled traditional rhymers have had to consider many subtle factors before choosing each rhyme. Modern poets tend to use rhyme, as they do rhythm, in an ever-shifting way. Sometimes I've read a poem and realized only afterward that it rhymed.

I tell kids I'd rather encourage other ways of writing, but if they love to rhyme they can use it where they think it fits.

ACROSTICS

> O how beautiful is the ocean. Why don't you
> Compare it to the fish's swimming motion?
> Even in a fishtank you can compare
> A fish's swimming motion. Even in a turtle
> Notion, you can find a fish's swimming motion.
> —*Percy Nunez, 6th*

Rhythm of second and third sentences (starting with lazy dactylic waves) matches content. Comparing the whole ocean to the motion of one of its parts (is a resident a part?) is a deep idea, taken further by the fishtank limit. And further yet, beautifully accompanied by a goofy, attention-drawing rhyme, in "turtle/notion...motion." Repetition, vowels, all swim.

> I
>
> Joy myself. I ate my
> Orange. I play in
> Sand. I
> Eat dinner. I
> Play outside. I
> Hit my friend.
> My mother cooks dinner.
> I ate my ice cream. I ate my
> Dinner. My
> Daddy can fix my bike. A cat
> Licks his fur. I ate my
> Egg. My dog has a
> Tail. My friend ate an
> Orange. I hammer a
> Nail.
> —*Joseph Middleton, 4th*

The grammatical spareness is soulful because extreme. It echoes the spareness of the commonplace events reported. The last sentence nails it all down. Due to the simple sentence structure, the line-breaks are rhythmically jagged.

> Lions
> In and
> Out of their cages.
> Nothing to do.
> —*Elissa Espis, 4th*

Economy snaps lightly shut.

> Some people
> Have
> A
> Picture in mind.
> Every one of us has
> Some kind of a shape nobody else has.
> —*Lillian Plaza, 5th*

Fine idea, like a mental fingerprint. Last line exemplifies, as well as speaks of, the necessary specificity, via rhythm.

> Pisces
> Is my
> Sign,
> Cool
> Every time. Can't
> Stop thinking why I'm so fine.
> —*Ana Grullon, 7th*

Streetswift. Long *i* in every line but one, a sharp, proclamatory sound. The rhythm sounds like cheerleading, which is what she's doing.

> Bouncing
> Along
> Like the ground was just there to
> Let it spring back into the air.
> —*Juan Martinez, 7th*

The rhythm naturally speeds up like the diminishing bounces of a free ball. Excellent idea ("ball-o-centrism") intensifies free spirit connected with ball. Also, the "there"/"air" rhyme amounts to a bounce from ground up.

> Lightning lights up the sky.
> In a second it's over.
> Gone forever, never the same.
> High in the sky,
> Through the air.
> Nothing more.
> In a second,
> Nothing there,
> Gone for good.
> —*Patrick Pouzier, 6th*

A list poem, really, a number of after-images of the lightning, each one a quick phrase, like lightning, each speaking of its absence while bringing it back.

> So tiny,
> Melted
> All the way down,
> Little,
> Little.
> —*Wayne Jackson, 7th*

Another list poem, this one of synonyms for the spine word "SMALL."
Everything emphasizes the smallness: "so," "all the way down" (which would
be the ultimate thinness of nothing), the lack of connective language. A jewel-
like shapeliness, with the only long line in the middle. "Little" has a much different effect the second time than the first; as Gertrude Stein has shown us,
there is no true repetition, the context being at least a little different each time.

> Disco music
> Ain't my style.
> Nice, soft music
> Could lift my feet to the
> Endless skyway.
> —*Leara Bowles, 6th*

The rhythm illustrates the sort of danceability she's after. The combination of
"ain't" with the nice, soft music and the extravagance of "endless skyway"
(perhaps borrowed from Woody Guthrie) shows us a particular person.

> Candle.
> Apron.
> Vapor.
> Evil.
> —*Alen Cepeda, 6th*

A very concise list, to the point that the plainest logic is still surprising. Progression in four trochees from human things to atmosphere to fright.

> Music is musical; it's really
> Unusual, you
> Sing and you play
> Instruments until all of your
> Cares are gone away.
> —*Angela Bryant, 5th*

Exaggerated lilt, with much alliteration and vowel-play, well illustrates the
subject.

PLACE POEMS

> Grenada coconuts, coconut water, rivers, crayfish, colorful blue
> seas, seaside grapes, fresh walnuts, fish, houses, beautiful
> freedom, nice beach, mangoes, pears, oranges, cherries, funny
> fruits and grapefruits.
> —*Temelle Peters, 4th*

Boldness of sheer list, randomness of moves within the list, give the feeling of
paradise-lying-around, the tropics. Read this poem aloud; the rhythm and
soundplay are like a brook dancing down to the sea.

TYPING ROOM

Click clack click clack as the keys go back
FGF space FGF space when the keys go back
The keys go back again and again and again
Sit back and straight
Fingers on the guide keys
Look at the chart
Pg 17 Supplementary Practice
When you finish put your hands on your
OK, let's start again
FGF space FGF space as the keys go back
As the keys go back
     —Jaye Slonim, 4th

Sophisticated sound abstract, mixed with other fact. The sound varies nicely between hard and soft (most strikingly in the move from line 8 to line 9). It's abstract but, paradoxically, concrete as no description could be.

LUNES

Down down down,
yellow and brown are falling
over the town.
     —Chris Leonardi, 4th

Efficient, pungent blend of visual and aural.

I'm in love.
I'm in love. Keep it
just like that.
     —Lisa Whittaker, 4th

Repetition necessary, even within the very short lune form, to give lyric contrast to the matter-of-fact last-sentence phrasing, which is thereby infused with emotion. Relative slowness of last line draws attention and a feeling of importance to itself.

Women are sexy.
Oh boy, is that true!
What'll I do?
     —Clarence, 6th

Description of content is made milder and rueful, thrown into perspective by rhyme-accentuated humor of "What'll I do?"

Rules are to
follow when you don't know
where to go.
     —Wanda Matos, 6th

Keen thought; syntax fits just right, almost slogan-neat. This quality is played with by the rhyme ("know"/"go") which, by not being an end-rhyme rhythmically, breaks the "rule" in suggesting it.

> My life is
> like New York, falling down
> in the dark.
> —*Edwin Fernandez, 8th*

Near rhyme ("York"/"dark"), comma to period. There are three long *i*'s, three short *i*'s, three *l*'s, three *n* sounds, three *k*'s, and two *d*'s gracefully lilting through this bit of talk. Mysterious poetic image as well.

> Sleeping very softly
> in my bed, dreaming of
> things in red.
> —*Joanna Stergiau, 5th*

Elegant, quiet slipping of a wild image (dreams full of red things) into the lulling rowboat rhythm established in the first two lines.

> My hands are
> up in the air but
> I don't care.
> —*Wanda Williams, 6th*

Simple pop-song sound harmonizes with lovely foolish picture: loveliness emerges slowly (in the reader's consciousness) from said sound.

> 1, 2, 3, 4, there's a girl in my class.
> 5, 6, 7, 8, she is pretty.
> 9, 10, 11, 12, she don't like me.
> —*Anonymous, 4th*

The humor of a perfect klunk sound points out music by direct opposition, like the ditty I once heard: "Roses are red/ violets are blue/ I have a lawnmower/ can you swim?"

> Read my palms,
> wrinkled future lines of love,
> different like doves.
> —*Sonia Polanco, 5th*

After the plainness of line 1, line 2 has high-energy rhythm, alliteration, and image ("wrinkled" a great word there) all tightly together. Line 3 keeps up the music but slows it, lets idea emerge.

> A beautiful thing,
> graceful piece of great art,
> Ballet Ballet Ballet.
> —*Regina Mack, 5th*

An elegant rhythm forms in first two lines, slows down due to complicated consonants and the spondee ("great art"), leaps ecstatically out of grammar in line 3.

> The sky is
> black. Not even a cat
> can see me.
>   —Mike Brown, 5th

Small thing put in perfect sound. Line 2 has lively rhythm, starts heavy repetition of nasal *a*, long *e*, terminal *t* and *n*. "See me" seems to me like a beam of light, trying to get there. A black cat is suggested but not really there.

> Goddesses are good
> and evil, living on a
> heavenly rocky star.
>   —Jon Fong, 6th

Classic picture livened by lyric energy of "heavenly rocky." Rich alliteration and vowel variety forms a matrix. A way to get better acquainted with the sound of a poem is to read aloud only the vowel sounds, then only the consonant sounds, and note their movements. Students enjoy hearing the resulting gibberish, and learn a little analysis.

> When I dress
> up, I dance around on
> my tippy toes.
>   —Carmen Vega, 5th

The isolated "up" seems to anticipate, in retrospect, the sudden tone-change of "tippy toes."

> Remember me, remember
> me. Put it all together
> and remember me.
>   —Nora Llerandez, 3rd

A beauty. "Put it all together" is a wonderful stroke to both balance and tie in with the repetition. The poem is line by line slow/fast/slow.

THING POEMS

> (*acrostic*)

> Sky, you are so blue and true.
> Kick down some rain or snow if
> You want to.
>   —Valerie Brown, 5th

Notice the rhythm of the rhyme. The spondaic energy of "kick down" contrasts with the soft relaxation of "blue and true." Try the "if" moved to line 3 and see how the effect becomes flaccid.

> Eggs are good, eggs are
> good. He never listened but he
> understood.
>   —*Dora Q., 3rd*

Simple rhythmic inevitability of a Mother Goose couplet, broken up to form interesting delayed rhymes, is used to give a provocative combination. The egg statement comes double, preparing the reader to think of the shell/life-source duality of an egg. "Good" contributes to this sense. Then the apparently disjunct last sentence can be taken as analogous—"never listened" as shell and "understood" as the life paradoxically sealed therein.

WILLIAM CARLOS WILLIAMS IMITATIONS

> I didn't mean to step on the cat,
> but she was so small she was smaller than a rat.
> I didn't mean no hurt, harm nor danger,
> but when I turned around she looked like a stranger.
>   —*Cheryl Bush, 5th*

The rhymes appear where you don't rhythmically expect them. Thus the spooky shock of "stranger" is intensified.

> beside the white shirt
> beside the white tie
> beside the dog and cat
> beside the fried chickens
>   —*Ralph, 4th*

"Beside the" is beside the progression of objects in more ways than one. Interesting that he picked "beside the" from the last line of Williams' poem to elaborate on, rather than "so much depends upon," and then divided the "white chickens" in two, coupling its elements to disparate images. I have no explanation for these moves but playfulness, which, united with "beside the," is not beside the point.

VARIOUS POEMS

> Off to the T to the T.I.E.
> Reggie Reggie at the T.O.P.
> The super lubba see ha see
> ig-u-stepa-wiba-stuba
> Not your mother or
> your father instant-instant-
> finga-chobba. If you wanna
> sabba lubba you won't
> see to wibba stuba. Super

lubba undercover Reggie
Reggie eat your brother.
    —*Leara Bowles, 5th*

Bop.

I like to see a tadpole;
I hate to see a sad soul.
First everything's plain,
then it starts to rain.
    —*Marquee Bonilla, 2nd*

Tight, obvious correspondences of rhyme and sentence structure, with links of meaning between lines 1 and 3 and between lines 2 and 4. "Everything's" and "it starts to" are thrown "against" each other, and it seems as if nature is all-inclusive but sadness is isolated, local. All slipped into an innocent brevity. A terrific piece.

"REAL-LIFE" PIECES

Saturday was a boring day.
It was so boring that I was boring of boring.
I took care of my boring niece.
I stayed in my boring house.
I ate my boring lunch.
I went out to the boring air.
I went out to a boring restaurant.
I bought boring food.
I looked at boring TV.
I washed boring dishes
and I fell asleep on my comfortable bed,
and the boring stuff came to be interesting.
    —*Barbara Diaz, 8th*

Insight of how excess of anything can be exciting, even excitement's opposite, through a sort of attitude overdose plus incantatory rhythm.

Waving "bye" to my folks. Scared by the minute. I was surrounded with love. So many things to do. Only doing one. Making a leak on the floor. Getting yelled at by my teacher. Drawing pictures that reminded me of outside. Playing with toys, sliding down the slide. Touching, seeing, hearing new things. Had a fight but might make up. Met a boyfriend so cute and nice, the only thing wrong is his name is messy? And going on to first grade leaving Mrs. Soldier like weaving a hatchet.
    —*Jackie DeSosa, 5th*

Stream of consciousness, keen and moving, incredible variety possible through that technique plus the fragmentary grammatical style. Each sentence moves on the basis of the previous one but into a new aspect of or overlap with it. So it travels around eventually tying together everything from the surrealism of "weaving a hatchet" ("waving" may have been meant, but "weaving" is there and provocative) to the most mundane bit. When a happy accident (such as "weaving" for "waving") occurs in adult composition, the artist often decides to keep it. One can point out the "mistake" to a child and give him or her the option of correcting or capitalizing on it.

> I remember my fish, gold with a spot of silver,
> diving up and down like a nighthawk.
> Once I came in the room; there he was
> floating on top. I cursed him out but he
> never moved. His graveyard was the toilet bowl.
> —*Collette Neils, 6th*

Beauty expressed in the colors and movements of the fish. The odd "once" as if this were only an interruption in the fish's existence, or in its relation to the poet. Then the sudden acceleration into toughness, the way we were taught to meet death. Outstanding sound, last line. "Toilet bowl" so isolated, after the *v*'s.

ABOUT POETRY

> Poetry is like a train going by so fast with a word of a poem on each car, which is like words from a poem going so fast through your head with many cars, 10, 11, with such beautiful words of a poem making it pretty, 21, 22, and some poems are as bright as a star and shooting as fast as a train and as dark as a train, 35, 36. Poetry is like a train writing a poem, shooting a lot of ink, 48, 49. Poetry can be frustrating like when a train passes and you're in your car at a crossing, 66, 67, and that is what I think about poetry.
> —*Alfred Olivera, 3rd*

Phillip Booth's poem "Crossing" adapted to a poetics. Apropos. Fast freight. The flow of the statements is effectively contrasted with the staccato sound of the numbers, like the speed vis-à-vis the clickety clack rhythm of an actual train. The poem loses power and becomes static in the last two "units."

> Poetry is just a ball that I'm throwing on the wall.
> —*John Young, 3rd*

Like the previous poem, appropriately inclusive of both thought and sound effects. The rhyme *includes* "wall," which is otherwise *outside* "poetry." Thus poetry is simultaneously specific and inclusive of that which it's played off of ("the world"?). The idea arises that poetry keeps returning to the mind, perhaps in unexpected ways, rather than being simply an outpouring of the known. 'Tis true, one line can cause a lot more talk than it gives.

> Poetry, poetry, I need a poetry.
> I want to learn about a poetry.

Someone told me it's like
a boy,
a girl,
my father,
my brother,
a scarecrow hanging on two sticks,
a toothpick,
a king,
a handsome guy,
a snake,
a snail,
a mopstick,
a star,
the wind,
the earth,
the moon.
　　　　　—Shawane Bryant, 5th

The dynamic variety of the list shows us that poetry may be present anywhere, on any level.

Poetry makes me happy
with a smile on my face
when I get that feeling I have to
solve the case.
　　　　　—Diana Rodriguez, 6th

"Solve the case" a sudden toughness within the smiling rhyme.

I remember writing a poem about writing a poem. And that poem was about writing a poem that I wrote about another poem and it went like this: I remember writing a poem about writing a poem. And that poem was about writing a poem that I wrote a long time ago.
　　　　　—Edward Lopez, 5th

Sophisticated variety within this Chinese box joke. It never falls into sheer repetition. "A long time ago" suddenly shrinks it all into perspective, like looking back at something from a departing airplane.

Chapter X

POETIC "MOVES"

"In our wildest dreams/ Our days are numbered"

The plural noun "moves" (as in "she's got a lot of moves in her line" or "good moves!") is used by many contemporary poets to designate a supple use of language in poems. It is more a matter of sophistication than the natural candor discussed in Chapter 6, there is a sense of the deliberate play of ideas and of the flavors and impacts of words, the dance of language, the image and idea counterpoint of sheer rhythm. I'm not referring here to the extremes of surrealistic play but to a writing situation wherein some kind of logical thread is evident but is not pushed to an all-consuming conclusion; rather the perceptions of the poet dance around it, play with meaning, create slants and surprises. In large part this simply amounts to a concentration on language and a love of language without letting it be dragged along by meaning, in a subservient role.

I believe the largest chasm of understanding between audience and poet is in their differing attitudes toward "meaning" in poetry. Readers seem to feel that a poem should wind up with a clear meaning, even that it should be paraphraseable with no loss in thought. This feeling is rooted in part in a natural resistance to the psychological revolution of the last 100 years, which has exposed the arbitrariness of much conscious proclamation and led to a greater interest and faith in the role of the subconscious in producing the elements of art. Even people who accept, or love, the distortions of Picasso and the abstractions of music may want their poetry made of noble ideas decoratively expressed. Such a double standard stems chiefly from the many other uses of language, mostly dominated by its use as an intellectualized mode of communication. It is hard for us to view language as a medium for art, since it's not so obviously visceral as sound and color.

But poetry is an art and must be allowed the same exactness in examining and then proportioning meaning and the same exploratory freedom that the other arts have. Techniques such as automatic writing, an extreme of letting (what one hopes to be) the subconscious mind dictate the work, have assumed places in the spectrum of literary approach; writers feel out their personal ways be- tween uncontrolled feeling and the guidance of the intellect, and are generally aware of a greater available range. And of course a new precision must be brought to bear on the words, since feelings are, in fact, as exact as anything.

So in this century the play of ideas has assumed a greater importance vis-à- vis ideas themselves, though a strong case could be made that, as far as the essentials go, "it was ever thus" in poetry; that is, that the key poetic qualities in, say, Shakespeare, the "lights" that bring his writings above others, and have made them for so long a time delightful, are the humors, the almost in- definable touches and turns, the inevitable surprises, of his instant-to-instant language (depending, of course, for their very life on the solid framework of his dramatic and character sense), and not his ideas, which are all derivative, at the service of his art rather than presented as any kind of gospel.

Moralistic approaches to literature can now be seen less as divine revelation than as society's survival techniques. This is not to denigrate such ap- proaches. A Pilgrim's Progress is still a delight across great gulfs of time and atti- tude, but not so much for its message as for the sheer vitality that Bunyan managed to bring to his form. The presence of a hard arbitrary form, the heroic couplet, in most of Alexander Pope's work certainly helped bring his language to its fiercely sharpened condition. The excitement of Hopkins would not be there without the strictures he both faithfully assumed and battled against. Without given forms and given ideas, modern artists must find and create their own "solids," and the impact of modern art has often been diffuse and defused for just such a lack.

The problems and the glory of modern art lie in the credit it gives to the flux of life rather than to the eternal verities. Each artist, indeed each twentieth- century person, tries to find his or her proper accomodation among the pulls of freedom and of discipline. And these pulls are not simply opposed to each other; the "psychic geometry" is much more complex.

Kids rarely think like all this. Nevertheless, they absorb, fully and delicately, the attitudes and struggles of their times, and when they write poetry it in- cludes, often with stunning clarity, concrete evidence of the most current as well as the most timeless human thought.

"Psychic geometry." By this I mean the way ideas arise for us, when reading a poem, and form a succession of shapes that interrelate. An example is third grader Anthony Pandazzo's lune:

> The sky has
> many clouds, birds, and pictures.
> My thoughts circle.

From "sky," "clouds," and "birds" we have a vast dome containing nebulous shapes and small, particular shapes. "Pictures" is then a different order of noun and can apply in a variety of ways: the suggestive shapes of clouds, por- tions of the skyscape, and, since "pictures" is in a list with clouds and birds, not mentioned in a way to include them, we may think of subtle variations in the sky itself or of visions we project onto the sky. "Pictures" implies a contemplating eye and mind and thus leads to "thoughts." The thoughts circle, which suggests the shape of the sky, choices between objects themselves and representations of them (pictures), the "many" things to look at, the movements in the sky, and the endlessness involved. The dome of the head becomes an analogue for the sky. The mind, circling, brings a scattered expanse of phenomena to a form (as the lune does). Such ideas have room to arise when the elements in the poem, however simple, are, first, chosen sensitively and then not forced into loaded contexts but left free to manifest their own roles in the poem.

Many children do have subtle qualities in their writings, abundantly, which traditional education has been slow to acknowledge. Since kids cannot usually maintain an equally subtle intellectual argument, their felt insights, as flashed in poems, are sometimes dismissed as incorrect, merely weird or at best accidental.

The distinction I feel between "moves" and surprise is simply that with the former the emphasis is not so much on a particular verbal leap, the breathless shock of that, as it is on just what has been moved from and what to, and how these combine to set up ongoing implications.

ACROSTICS

Hundreds
Of
Lines all around, all
Empty.
—*Victor V., 3rd*

Psychic geometry: the expression of hole by multiplicity of its surroundings, and the sense of the surroundings being sucked dry by the hole's presence. Repetition of "all" gives breadth to the emptiness too.

Dancing by myself I feel like I'm on air.
In the sky I can dance all day.
And I come down from the sky and tell my brother,
"Nice to be dancing with someone you know,
Even when you are dancing by yourself."
—*Diane Fludd, 7th*

"By myself," "on air," "in the sky," and "all day" build up the isolation. "Come down" makes one try to picture the descent, entices but withholds an exact picture. Usually details help, but in this case such specific words as "tumble" or "slide" would only distract from the loneness of the dance. Choice of brother as confidant seems meaningful, close but far. "Nice" is a charm of informality, and she is beside herself with poise, half in company, half alone.

Come
And see a

Rose.
Oh it's
Like
I
Now know
Enough.
   —Caroline Baez, 4th

After "Rose," the poem leaps to a mental geometry in which the last two lines
are like petals. Examine the vowels from "Oh" to "Enough" and the *n* alliteration at the end. Very pretty music, dovetailing neatly with the ideas, the mirror effect of "Like" and the beauty of knowing "Enough."

Open your mind to the
Universe, and
Run back home and get your lunch.
   —Juan Lugo, 7th

A hollowness in very large thoughts is exposed by the humorous mundanity of
line 3. This deflation is "our" lot in life, he seems to say. The suddenness of the
leap would normally put this poem in the "surprise" category but for the emphasis on meaning. It may also mean, more straightforwardly, that it will take a
while to study the universe.

Seeing the days
Coming and going.
Outside the gray blue sky,
Races and traces all in our
Places.
In our wildest dreams
Our days are numbered.
   —Rosario Fernandez, 6th

The first five lines set up a mood of metaphysical song, hinting at oppositions
Then the last sentence is a beautiful triumph of delicate balance between *nearly* opposite ideas. Lines 6 and 7 are both clichés, but together they become new
and powerful.

PERIOD

Pacing every sentence,
Erasing every meaning,
Riding always at the end,
In and out of things, the
Outstanding point never
Dies.
   —Richard Suarez, 6th

It would take many times the poem's length, books even, to trace out the implications that may arise from the verbs in this poem, the in-and-out nature of
the period, its immortality, the very focus on it. If a period "never dies," does
that mean its qualities of rhythm ("pacing"), destruction ("erasing"), terminat-

ing, and recurring are immortal?

> People
> Order me around
> East and west, so
> Me and myself hit the road.
> —*Kaisha White, 5th*

Independence/fellowship-with-self of poet, hitting the road instead of going prescribed directions. The "poem" (the spine word) is the vehicle, not the poet (self), a good insight in this rebellion.

> What
> Are
> Legs?
> Legs are legs.
> —*Marquee Bonilla, 1st*

The barrier in our mobility. Ontological gesture from a first-grader. If this seems unlikely, consider a bright six-year-old putting down "WALL" and feeling his way to an opposite sense, legs, suggested by the L, then getting a taciturn feeling, carried from "wall" into the legs, as a sort of play, and saying "Legs are legs."

> Jack will
> Understand
> Love and
> I will not
> Allow it.
> —*Julia Papleo, 3rd*

She has the good insight that understanding is not a cure-all, contains power that needs monitoring. "Not/Allow it" is great, with defiant anxiety edging in via real speech.

> Lory is my friend.
> Oh, what a day. The
> Violin is playing.
> End of story.
> —*Joanne Liriano, 3rd*

A "story" from juxtaposition alone, the three elements culminating in a lovely aural afterimage.

> A
> Neat
> Doubt.
> —*Richard H., 6th*

The connective exposed as not containing the specificity that faith requires.

> Looking
> Over the

Ocean,
Praying at the sky.
—*Maribel Cairo, 4th*

Wondering how she thought to use "loop" is a bafflement and a pleasure. The action here does form a loop, a great spiritual loop of seeing water (source of life) and praying in air.

LUNES

My pattern goes
round and round until it
decides to stop.
—*Lucinda Leung, 4th*

Pictorialization of how one's "pattern" (self) circles about until it (rather than our conscious minds) fixes on something. Again, the student may not have "thought" this, but she felt it.

I love TV.
I love when they zoom.
That's my style.
—*Lina Cetrulo, 5th*

Line 1 plain. Line 2 cute wording ("love when they"). Line 3 hip, set off especially by the change from the two "I love's."

A dream is
like watching TV—the problem
is being inside.
—*Mayra Reyes, 6th*

"Problem"—you can't get out—like the possible claustrophobia of this short form. But it doesn't seem too bad, only a problem, and one thinks of the eventual problems of the problem-free TV.

The mouth is
a hole in the face
that moves gracefully.
—*Pandora Stone, 8th*

The change of tone between lines 2 and 3 is extreme without skipping a beat. Smooth ride from beast to beauty.

The above three poems illustrate different types of line-breaks that come up in lunes. Lina's emphasizes the line structure (three/five/three), and its musical qualities, by making line correspond to sentence. Mayra's plays with the structure by breaking it in the very midst of grammar. This draws the reader's attention to effects in the tiniest units of speech (for example, the heaviness of "is" at line's end relative to its placement at the beginning). Pandora's poem glides through the lines, especially lines 2 and 3, thereby setting

97

off their contrast.

> A picture lights
> up a life to living
> on the earth.
> —*Noah, 4th*

Seeing a picture can change the way one sees life. This seems to say we can approach reality via representation, a good insight that validates art. Interesting sound centered in line 2.

> Why do I
> look at my mother's mirror
> all the time?
> —*Shirley, 3rd*

Last line shifts it into overdrive, or, tiny rocket stages to the ego.

> The woman is
> pretty for you, but whatever
> happened to me?
> —*Nneka Thomas, 6th*

Line 1 sets up. Line 2 has prettiness of sound and subject. Line 3 snaps it off. Typical lune dynamics.

> I'm on the
> phone a lot, making arrangements
> to go places.
> —*Jennifer, 4th*

"A lot" plus the pretentious tone of "making arrangements" plus the feeble hopefulness of "to go places" make this like the bravado of a doll about to crack. Such tone-progressions are well within the intentional range of kids.

THING POEMS

> Piece of paper not hollow
> Piece of paper flat on my desk
> Piece of paper sitting there just plain flat
> Piece of paper that I'm writing on
> Piece of paper with lines all over it
> Piece of paper have a heart that you don't have
> Piece of paper I need you to write
> Piece of paper all over the school
> Piece of paper you drive me Capupso
> Piece of paper I love you
> Piece of paper you're everywhere
> Piece of paper good luck, you'll die with a smile
> Piece of paper the world needs you
> Piece of paper I need to write you.
> —*Ana Roman, 4th*

A chant, emerging in a "poem about things" assignment, with a rich range of imaginative variation. The clause "...good luck, you'll die with a smile" is especially wild and felicitous. Just for one thing, one thinks of a piece of paper curling up (smile) when burnt, the clearest death for paper.

> By the way hair comes out in the morning, it describes the experi-
> ence you could have had during the night.
> —*Priscila Leon, 8th*

"Comes out" is the perfect verb form, with its dual meanings of emerge and result, and "could have had" seems to hint at dream, without denying the chance of "real" adventure.

WILLIAM CARLOS WILLIAMS IMITATIONS

The following adaptations of the "red wheelbarrow" idea depend chiefly on the dynamics of simple progressions of images. As in a rapid slide show, the moves overlap and leap.

> So much depends upon
> the glazed light in the
> night and the cool fresh
> air. The drinking fountain.
> The map. A sandwich.
> The big marching band.
> —*Charles Forbes, 4th*

> An important thing is
> a sock with a hole in it,
> a zoo with no animals in it,
> an animal with no mouth,
> a girl cutting your hair,
> a candy bar with no candy in it,
> clothes to wash,
> me and my brother, my mother and father,
> a candle burning.
> —*Papri Garkar, 3rd*

> It all depends upon
>
> a red bleeding
> heart flower
>
> a flock of
> wild geese
>
> some broken cars
> —*Anthony L., 3rd*

> So much depends upon
> the green grass

growing and the evening
standing up high
        —*Marc Edwards, 5th*

Some clocks are bells.
And some clocks are paper.
And some papers are doors.
And doors are shows.
Shows are water.
Water is a basket.
A basket is a picture.
A picture is a hanger.
A hanger is outside.
Outside is my friend.
        —*Donna Nesbitt, 3rd*

So much depends upon
the dead dog on the
sidewalk
a building on fire
down the street
the lives of the people on the street
walking around.
        —*Kenya Askew, 5th*

So much depends
upon
a little red Corvette
a big dog chasing me
raindrops falling on my window
the sun drying the rain
        —*Michael Kasper, 5th*

So much depends upon
a tree with green leaves
water falling from the sky
and you beside the car
        —*Wendy Hernandez, 5th*

VARIOUS POEMS

My boyfriend and I did the hop and twist,
with my new skirt and saddle shoes.
My skirt with the poodle on it twirled up.
I sat at one of the booths
and looked around.
A malt shop with team pennants.
Tomorrow I was going to the Sock Hop.
Chubby Checker came on with "Let's Do the Twist."
My boyfriend called, "Come on," and I
danced.
        —*Denise Smith, 6th*

Sophisticated. A variety of movements, well graphed. Varied line lengths climaxing in perfect lone "danced." The feeling overall seems delicately poised between loneliness and acceptance of that world. Line 6 (the indefinite article, the selection of corny images) injects a little sardonic perspective into the "Happy Days" scene.

> The sun is like a rose
> People said a rose could never be the sun
> and I said yes! yes! yes!
> And I kept saying yes!
> —Kaisha White, 5th

Breathtaking lyric moves, especially in the simple affirmative shout. Here the large thing is "like" the small and the small is shouted into being the large, not just being like it. Oddness of imagining "people" saying what she says they said.

"REAL-LIFE" PIECE

> I was having a science lesson about the Earth. And while my teacher was turning it I stared at it and it looked like a spool of thread and then it turned into a big ball. And then it was a satellite and then it was a big balloon and the big pen popped it. And that was the end of my lesson. And I came out of the school and played tag.
> — Michael Gattuso, 3rd

After the identity of the Earth has metamorphosed from thing to thing, in imagination, during the "science lesson," and been properly popped at the end (deflated by the hard scientific scrutiny of the "big pen"), the narrator plays, of all things, tag, the perfect physical analogue for his mind trip.

ABOUT POETRY

> Poetry is like a dream that should come true but still lies in its
>   place.
> Poetry is like walking on the moon with the flow of going
>   backwards and the motion of going forward.
> —Richard Cox, 6th

Striking psychic geometry, dynamizing stillness in line 1 and then picking apart flow and motion, springing them to opposition.

> Poetry is a fast train. You can't catch it and it disappears and you
> have to wait for the next train. And it comes and it disappears.
> You get so mad you fly to the moon.
> —Abdalla Hassan, 4th

The Great Escape. The idea that true imaginative flight is by unexpected vehicles.

> When I write a poem I
> feel I'm on a hot beach
> and the cool air flows
> over. With the lifeguard
> blowing his whistle.
> —*Litsa Tsiavo, 6th*

Into the dichotomous setup, of hot solid and cool flow, the whistle penetrates, sharp as language can be.

> Poetry is like raindrops, it hits you one at a time.
> Poetry is like a falling star, it comes when you're not expecting it.
> Poetry is like a sign on a store window that goes off and on.
> —*Anthony Bartley, 3rd*

In the lines are exemplified, respectively, focus, surprise, and rhythm—three basics of poetry indeed.

Chapter XI

THE POETRY OF FACT

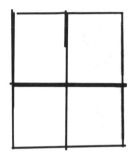

"A boy rides by on a silver bike"

Show-don't-tell is a familiar principle of creative writing—and indeed of anything we do, from love to auto mechanics. It means that one should exemplify rather than explain or merely describe. One must re-create the life observed and cannot depend on summarizations such as "the day was beautiful," since each reader will bring his or her own prefabricated set of mental details to such generality; thus nothing more substantial than a reminder will be given. One re-creates by accumulation of sensory details, by reproducing speech patterns, by taking the time to build in words the *atmosphere* one has in mind.

Like all principles it cries out for modification, even violation, in actual practice. The imperfection of the principle lies chiefly in the fact that after all it's all right to tell, especially when you "show" too.

If we imagine the various poetic qualities, such as rhythm, concision, and show-don't-tell, to be the facets of a single crystal, we can see how they overlap. By putting the crystal in a certain light, any one facet can be seen by itself. Show-don't-tell is adjacent to "moves" on this hypothetical crystal. They each tend to play with details that are images from the so-called objective world. But whereas the language "moves" a poet employs tend to emphasize the mental climate or mental geography of the poet, show-don't-tell is a simple, specific dictum — aimed at correcting a widespread fault of excessive abstraction — that encourages the writer to create full pictures of the "real world."

Show-don't-tell is a basic focus children need to be taught, especially for writing. Though children have, once they start using it, the fresh eye for what's going on, they typically tend to overlook the communicative necessities of language. They assume their reader (or listener) will automatically imagine the scene in all its details, and so they summarize experience quite blankly. "I went to the store. Then I came back and watched TV." The generality of such words, leaving out detail to an extreme, can be an attractive style at times. Nevertheless, most richness of expression is found after learning to make a very dogged effort to detail matters. With time, or inspiration, one learns how to select so as to bring out essences, though it never becomes a mere technique. In any case, one needs to impress upon children, by statement and by example, that their reader/hearer starts with zero, and they have to create carefully, and from scratch, the little world they have in mind, that relying on old formulae is just a lazy dodge. Poetry demands that one *think hard* about what one has to give in words, whether it takes two seconds or two years.

This book is a "show *and* tell." I despair of making the balance fit, as in a poem. It is only on the normal human shoulders of a lot of typical ten-year-olds, with their flashes of genius, that I've dared to essay what I essay.

ACROSTICS

Sun shines down at us.
Under the flowers I see ladybugs.
My sister and I are playing around.
Milkweed is growing out of the ground.
Enormous bears and tiny bugs
Roam the forest around us.
    —*Semyon Veytsman, 3rd*

Nature tinged with fairytale, the latter mostly through the enormous roaming bears, the flavor of old Europe that those tales convey. Also giving dimension are the macro/micro moves ("sun" to "bugs," etc.), the freedom from "summer" clichés, and the freshness of the milkweed line.

Pull the pigtail.
I did!
Go on, pull it!
Tease her.
Amuse her.
I did!
Let her run home to Mommy.
    —*Kristina Lacognata, 4th*

Showing a vivid three-way conflict through dialogue alone.

When the moon is full
Enter your house,
Read with calm,
Eat in peace, but
Watch out for the Wolfman
Out in the yard
Looking at you
From behind the fog.
    —*Anthony Fraticelli, 6th*

Not a touch of violence, much peace in fact, but plenty ominous, especially the word "fog," which emits maximum spookiness due to the delicate buildup. This is a poem I find so economical, yet so successful and expressive of atmosphere, I've used it a thousand times in class as the introductory acrostic example.

> Under the artificial me which
> No one really knows, I try to
> Deliver the message that I hope
> Everyone will see. What is
> Right or wrong. I am
> Starting to find out.
> Trying to know which one I should do;
> Although I am confused and
> No one is listening and I am almost near
> Death,
> I'm trying to
> Nervously tell
> God to fill me with understanding.
> —Jane Martinez, 8th

Although this poem speaks outright of its large subject throughout, the main effect is via the line lengths, summed up in the word "nervously," plus a sincere tone, rather than in explication. A terrific piece; the passion has room to be very large.

> Teachers give us
> Easy work.
> Ai! They waste their time.
> Cat
> Hat
> Eat
> Rat.
> —Melissa Villanueva, 6th

A pure exaggerated form of showing.

> Lying in bed
> All alone. It's scary in the
> Night all by myself, and then a
> Goblin goes into my room
> Unseen by me
> And then I see him
> Grab me and take me away from the
> Entrance.
> —Ruvane, 4th

The poem, with its passivity, isolation, and spooks in and out of visibility, seems to portray the superstitious darkness clustered before the entrance to language.

> Oceans
> Cooling,

Everyone yelling
And kneeling on the sand like
Nothing ever happened.
    —John Chang, 6th

A great disproportion in time casts things clear into other dimensions. We
don't apprehend as time that which takes much more than a lifetime; we
assume as permanent that which in a larger perspective is transitory. The poet
chose a perfect "show" example for this, the ocean and beach.

PLACE POEMS

THE TREE HOUSE

When I look down
at my dog he looks
like a boat turned over.
I have apple all over me,
and the air is so sweet.
It is like flying in the air.
I sit down and relax to look at the birds.
    —Claudia Claudio, 4th

Picture of the dog from above is a great locating image. "Apple all over me"
beautifully gets the tree-house air. Following lines lift it up more. But how
could someone named Claudia Claudio fail? The last line, being so believable
and soft and yet scrupulously heavenly, especially excites, given the ladder of
words that led there.

CONEY ISLAND

At the cotton candy stand
I watch the man make it.
Adding the sugar!
  Red, yellow, blue!
And the smooth sugary
feeling going down my
throat! Standing on the
hot ground. Walking down
the Boardwalk ready to
plunge into the water.
    —Ruth Morales, 5th

Fine variety of physical expressions. The "standing" sentence solidifies the
whole picture especially (extends the focus from just eyes and mouth). The
music of verbs and object nouns in the last seven lines grounds the tasty situation.

My room is a mess.
My sister's clothes are lying around.
Her shoes are all over the ground.

Her perfume bottles are open,
making the room smell like an Avon store.
My clothes are all hung up in the closet.
My perfume is all shut tight so that I can't
even open it myself.
            —Romelia Leach, 5th

MY ROOM

Noisy place
Wallpaper of flowers all over
Sitting on my bunk bed eating
Froot Loops day and night
Looking at my bureau
With Avon Blush on
Top of my Cover Girl Mascara
Next to my Tinkerbell Powder
And my lightbulb mirror
Also looking at my closet, at
All the clothes I have
At the bottom are my 16 pairs of shoes
            —Jackie Angulo, 8th

PUERTO RICO

Sun burning on the ground.
Flowers blooming every place.
Beautiful beaches with roaring waves. So big and beautiful.
Little crabs floating on the water.
White birds with brown necks, looking like leaves floating in
      the air.
Such a wonderful place to be under the burning sun.
Free as clouds.
Smell the fresh air.
Puerto Rico.
            —Petrouchka Mendez, 4th

Romelia's poem works chiefly via a tight revelation (emotional but done with fact) at the end, a turnaround on the attitude preceding it—her neatness has closed things off for her. Jackie's develops flavor of place through the charm of flowery names. The exactness of them becomes funny by the time we get to the mirror. Petrouchka's adds up large geographical glories tersely expressed, in expansive words, and in the middle zeroes in on the crabs and birds with their caught details and to the one comparison in the poem, "looking like leaves," which stands out by having been "rationed" as the details stand out in the more general pictures around them. So we have, A, a dramatic climax, B, a texture throughout, and C, a focus in its larger context, just some of the ways to show more than is told.

THE RIVER

Bottles bobbing up and down,
Torn paper packages spinning.
Thinking peaceful thoughts while
Looking down at the horrible river.
Trying to look through the filth
And grey, beaten garbage,
Wondering what is down below.
Thoughts of scenes from
Movies of underwater
Where beautiful big blue fish swim.
Wondering if this could be down in
This ugly river where bottles
Bob and packages spin.
            —Elizabeth Vazquez, 7th

Details show. At the same time she's not afraid to use the word "horrible," which would seem uncool to many adult poets, nor to imagine pretty underwater movies. These reactions help make her poem human and believable, not just a tract. The thought of "beautiful big blue fish" moving under the garbage is thrilling.

CAMPING

I wondered if it would be fun.
But then I got used to it,
I knew my way around.
Looking in the shallow waters,
Sun reflecting light.
Then it was time to go home.
As I was leaving, it sounded like
the shallow waters were saying good-bye.
            —Eleuterio Olmeda, 5th

BEACH

Waves crashing on the rocks.
Jelly fish sliding under your feet.
The water so calm and warm.
Sun shining bright in your eyes.
The wind blowing through your hair.
Then the rain falls and your day
rolls away like the tide.
            —Leslie Santiago, 5th

Eleuterio's poem fixes on one aspect of the camping—the stream—and lets the light from it stand for the understanding he got of the place ("I knew my way around") and the sound of it stand for farewell. Leslie's poem builds up a sense of the place by mentioning many details, then finishes with the beautiful comparison of tide and time in the last line ("rolls away").

LUNES

I saw you
talking to your best friend
in the park.
—*Eulalia Batista, 5th*

Since they are quite alive to the nuances of the feelings they have, kids interpret this simple snapshot to be eleven words of jealousy.

The wind is
blowing as I stand waiting
for my love.
—*Anonymous, 4th*

The wind expresses physically the insecurity of waiting.

When we walk
at night, we're scared — robbers
in the air.
—*Andrew Bernier, 7th*

A one-punch poem: "in the air" gives the palpability that special ghostliness.

Peas are what
I hate, but peas are
what I eat.
—*Deanna Fernandez, 6th*

"That's life" in a grain of pea. Line-breaks contrast humorously with the dead-center straightforward utterance.

The color of
the wall staring at me
all day long.
—*Javier Perez, 4th*

Javier may have come to this on his own, but the piece seems too standardly "poetic," the sensitive fragment. One half-expects an ellipsis after "long." If a specific color had been mentioned, the mystery would be reduced to a workable proportion.

"REAL-LIFE" PIECES

ROLLER-SKATING

I seemed like a gold blur beating against the air,
rolling down a hill with greased lightning everywhere,
reflecting my rays of joy
with speed of flash
and the thrill of the future, and when I fell, wow, squash!

I almost fainted with all the excitement of being mashed.
I started to fly with
amazement and fear.
I came down in about a year.
    —Anonymous, 6th

Rich, original metaphors and usages: "gold blur," "beating against the air," "with greased lightning everywhere," "thrill of the future," "wow, squash," going off into jolly, outrageous rhymes, "squash"/"mashed" and the last couplet, very sassy, all this showing to a tee the colorful energy of skating. "Rays of joy," "speed of flash," "almost fainted," "fly" threading the richness with headlong motion.

On Christmas Day I went outside and it was snowing and I built a snowman. I went upstairs to get a red button and two black ones, a hat, a scarf, three little balls and two sticks. I put the hat on his head. I took the three balls and put them on the snowman's belly and I took the red button and put it on for a nose. The two black buttons were his eyes. When I was finished I felt like a gentle breeze through my hair. I went upstairs, everybody was opening gifts. I had a lot of gifts but the best one was making a snowman.
    —Deyanira Alvarez, 4th

Very nice piece, the how-to facts and then the gentle breeze. The last sentence, which should be omitted, is an example of the desire, cribbed from adults, to explain the meaning, as if a good poem doesn't give it sufficiently, or as if explanation were superior to expression. Such homiletic co-optings of the poem's material merely suck away its energy. Everybody "opening gifts," in this case, expresses a mild irony just fine to end with as is.

On Friday at 3 o'clock Olga came to my house. We were both wearing our uniforms. We went into my blue room and changed into our ballet clothes. I was wearing red and Olga was wearing blue. At 4 o'clock we went to Burger King. Olga had a Whopper Jr. and I had a regular hamburger. Then we went to a shabby old store and bought 2 bags of cheeze doodles. We ate most of the cheeze doodles. We went inside to class and took off our jeans and put on our ballet slippers. My slippers were gold and Olga's slippers were pink. We went to the cold gray bar and started to dance. The music was slow, slow as a turtle. Then we did the dance, it was slow too. Then we went to our bags and put on our tap shoes and started to dance fast, fast as a jackrabbit. Then we were finished. We got dressed and left. It was snowing very lightly. I walked Olga home. It was dark and gloomy. I went home and ate lamb stew. Then I went in my blue room and did my homework. I went to bed.
    —Kathy Crespo, 5th

Judy Blume material through Piet Mondrian lenses. The exactitude ("lamb stew") helps create a little world.

JUNKIES

The dopers are out, the smokers are out.
They stand on the corner and wait.
They wait for more drugs and stand in the cold.
They pose and stand and grunt in pain
Just standing there. I think I'm
going insane. They go on their trips
every hour of the day.
What can anyone say?
They wear any old clothes from head
to their toes; they're always eating
something sweet; I don't have anything
against them, but frankly
they give me the creeps.
  —Anonymous, 7th

Sunday I went to the cemetery and to White Castle. The
cemetery was very foggy because it was raining, so the grass and
the sand turned into mud, so we didn't get out of the car. We saw
my grandmother's grave from the car. And then we left to go to
White Castle and we bought 25 hamburgers, 5 chocolate shakes, 3
onion rings and 2 french fries. It was me, my cousin, my aunt, my
mother and my uncle. Then we left. I had the time of my life.
  —Elizabeth Cotto, 8th

In "Junkies" the moderate quality of actual knowledge (standing in the cold,
"any old clothes," eating sweets) allows a more telling portrayal than fiery rhet-
oric would; they seem pitiable. Elizabeth's piece uses facts and an ongoing rhythm to unite feelings that in the conventions of exposition would be hard to
blend. That is, she simply shows us the visit to her grandmother's grave and the
fast-food feast, so close in time, without comment. The cliché emotions connected with death would be too ready to spring out were there any explanation.

Well, Saturday I started a report
on George Washington Carver.
It was kind of hard but I finished it
on time. George Washington Carver
was born in 1859 in Diamond Glove, Missouri.
He studied at Simpson College. When
I was writing this report I was
eating candy while writing and listening
to the radio. Disco music was playing
on the radio, it took me an hour to finish
writing this report on George Washington
Carver. I live in the public buildings
named after him.
  —Lisa Ramos, 8th

A graceful blend of thought and its surroundings, each putting the other in
perspective.

A lady was screaming for joy.
Her scream was very surprising and very emotional too.
When the lady screamed her nose and mouth kind of crinkled a
   little.
Her nose was as red as an apple; we can also say as red as a
   tomato.
The lady's scream sounded just exactly like the scream of a bird.
She had a pair of new boots on that looked like two bananas on
   her feet, moving from side to side.
The boots were very pointy.
There was such a bad wind that when I looked at her hair it
   was popping up as if she had seen a strange creature.
   —*Evelyn Garcia, 8th*

Unmerciful analysis of the physical by-products of joy.

I remember
when I saw
a piece of
paper on past air
and I ran after
it and I bumped
into a fat man
and he was so
fat he took a
whole sidewalk
and I lost my
piece of paper and
I saw a pizza
parlor and went
inside and ate one
with everything
on it and I
forgot all about it.
   —*Patricia Cruz, 5th*

The low key of the events (and their expression) tends to make the paper (what was on it?), the fat man, and the pizza with "everything" loom large symbolically, since our minds typically search for significance and can find it here only in these ordinary matters. Thus transience is poignantly expressed.

A bird lying in the middle of the street.
A blue car riding over, then another and another.
Nobody gives a second glance.
A dog sniffs at it, then scampers away.
A baby is crying screaming.
The sun is hitting off a window and
gleaming in the street.
A boy rides by on a silver bike.
It started to rain and washed the whole scene away.
   —*Caryn Gill, 8th*

The scene is mundane (though not exaggeratedly so—"blue" and "baby" have connotations of rising) and from that the sun's reflection begins to rise (though still tied to a window) and then the silver moving bike carries it into romance. The washing-away by rain (as if rain washes away scenes) is a neat additional touch, a second climax, lifting the imagery to fantasy.

> I was walking down the street when I was coming from the park
> when all of a sudden I looked down and saw a baby sparrow. I
> picked it up and put it in a bag and took it home. It was the color of
> fall leaves falling on the ground. I gave it food and water but the
> next week it flew out the window. I wondered where it had gone.
> —*Julian Vargas, 6th*

Simple narrative illuminated in the middle by the lovely metaphoric description, without which the tale would be gray, the movement plain.

ABOUT POETRY

> Poetry is like a haunted house getting frightened by another
> haunted house.
> Poetry reminds me of a cat washing itself while the master is
> looking for it.
> —*Anonymous, 5th*

Line 1 a double remove into spirit, line 2 similar but done via a "real" scene.

> Poetry is like a breath in the air.
> Poetry is a hard thing, like a weight on my head.
> Poetry is like a bumpy world.
> Poetry is like a rainstorm just standing there.
> —*Lillian Lopez, 5th*

From breath (lightly, magically there) to personally localized hardness, then that spreading, "head" to "bumpy world." Then you see its paradoxical stillness and transparency and it's almost full circle.

> Poetry is like your hand is coming apart.
> Poetry makes your mind look like a kingsize bay.
> Poetry reminds me of a heart in your mind that beeps.
> —*Evan Davis, 5th*

Parts of the self getting metamorphosed, or exposed, by poetry. Line 1 can be seen as the functional losing its usual functions. Line 2 an original way of expressing largeness, in a sense of breadth more than "depth." Line 3 union of thought and feeling, with the latter calling the shots.

> Poetry is like your mouth playing a trick on you.
> —*Nanette Suarez, 3rd*

Inspiration, the sense of gift from your non-intellectual self, without any goody-goodiness.

Poetry is like a rainbow with no colors.
Poetry is like biting into a hard cookie.
Poetry is like going horsy back riding.
Poetry is like putting your shoe on the wrong foot.
Poetry is like sitting in mud.
Poetry is like raw steak.
    —Jenene Mulholland, 5th

Comparisons showing poetry as tough, uncivilized, down-to-earth. A nice heterogeneity of images.

Poetry is like a cloud rolling down. Poetry is like the moon falling down. Poetry is like my hand falling off. Poetry is like a person floating in the air. Poetry is like a banana going away in the wind. Poetry is like a monkey saying "take me away!" Poetry is like a smile in the air. Poetry is happiness. Poetry Poetry is like a going-away trip. Poetry is like a zoo of heads. Poetry is like money in the air. Poetry is like coins floating. Poetry is like a silver dollar in the air. Poetry is like songs in my mind. Poetry is like a floor in the moon. Poetry is like the rain going in the sun. Poetry is like books in a pool. Poetry is like a mouse. Poetry is like an eagle in the air. Poetry is like cherries in the ears. Poetry is like poetry. Poetry is like desks in a door. Poetry is like a queen. Poetry is like a light going out.
    —Filomena Clemente, 2nd

Seven "disappearances" in the first seven sentences; everything's there and not-there. A sense of richness, that comes and goes, from a second-grader.

Writing a poem is like a fly that writes poems. It goes in your ear, it throws a bombful of poems, it blows up and makes you feel KOKO Bom Bom.
        When it makes me so KOKO Bom Bom, I turn into a fly and do it to you.
    —Norman Ortiz, 5th

Beneficial Dracula-style infection, ear rather than throat, and a more nearly invisible winged creature.

Poetry is like the alphabet all talking at once.
    —Kristina Lacognata, 4th

Tower-of-Babel energy obscures meanings (but they're there).

Poetry is like a glass,
one small mistake
and you lose it.
Poetry is like water
so many things underneath
it really doesn't end.
    —Alfred Nunn, 5th

Poetry as fragile but endless, and the endlessness consists not in itself but in what lies "under" it.

> Poetry is like
> seeing the
> sky without a
> color and
> watching all the
> birds flying
> without wings.
> —*Lourdes Nunez, 6th*

Again, beauty and absence, lovely zero made pictorial.

> Poetry is like a stampede of cows
> running in my mind, coming in one
> ear, going out the other.
> —*Irena Chaplin, 4th*

Almost the same as above, but speaking of poetry's power this time instead of its beauty.

> Poetry is like
> having a snake
> in your room
> and you don't know what to do.
> —*Lisa Colon, 6th*

Deadly visualization of the dangers of art, plunging into uncontrollable areas of the spirit. Combination of form (near-rhyme, tight rhythm) and the burst of sound at the end (well expressing the meaning) exemplifies the stress of the poem. A conclusive show-don't-tell.

Chapter XII

CONNECTIONS: METAPHOR AND SURREAL LANGUAGE

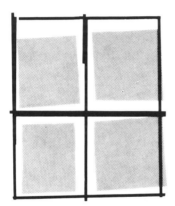

"When I put my shoes on, the sky turned peach and brown"

You have to be truly inspired to teach the uses of metaphor. All too often it (and its cousin, simile) is overemphasized in class-room approaches to poetry, and becomes too cut and dried as a device, too mechanical a mode of comparison. A cloud is like (blank). Ans.: a ball of cotton. Such excessive, predetermined neatness boxes in inspiration without air to breathe. Such reliance on formulae for the movement of images and thought (as opposed to, say, the acrostic, which pretty much leaves content open) leads to the one-on-one symbolism ("The white spider in Frost's poem stands for divine purity") that tends to reduce the educated understanding of poetry.

But in its broader sense metaphor is what connects one thing to another for us in poems. Unifying our scattered perceptions is *very* basic to poetry, which is why we shouldn't allow metaphor to be arbitrary or formulaic. Children, when using metaphor without a prescription, tend either to use it so blatantly as to cast it into a humorous perspective or to let it crop up naturally in their writings.

One lone metaphor can stand out as a concentrated point of reference out-side the poem's nominal subject, like the "mistake" in a Navajo woven basket traditionally put in to let the spirits pass in and out. A sea of metaphor can organically give some sense of the interconnectedness of all things.

I prefer, as a serious tool, metaphor that is not mechanically isolated but a comparison grammatically and otherwise woven into the surrounding elements of the poem. Metaphor that does not say, this is that, period, bingo, but lets the comparison gather and fray and be not quite explained.

As metaphor connects things outside the mind, surreal language connects the mind to the world outside it, in addition to the ways that common logic does. What I call surreal here could be termed "mixed." There's nothing new under the sun, but there are new combinations. The shocks of dream and the originalities of imagination are always based on new combinations of old things. For example, limpness by itself is ordinary; a watch is ordinary. But when Salvador Dali began including limp watches in his imaginary landscapes he provided an all-too-clear token for what the surreal is. A tiny blue giraffe, with shaving-cream eyes, dancing the black bottom is a tossup of simple elements, easy really—just rack your brains for visual things that don't match, stick 'em together. Many kids fall into the trap of stopping there, pasticing up a surface goofiness, but the surreal draws its power from the logic of wildness, the combinations that are felt, not just thought up, that come, however unprecedented, from real, subconscious juxtapositions. Waiting for these, or carefully seeking to stir them up, is the patience the poet needs.

Though they are violations of rational patterns, all serious surreal connections, when looked at long, seem to move toward meaning. We can, as poets or teachers, spread a mistaken emphasis on neatness of thought by insisting on a premature completion of these moves toward meaning. If a poem seems to hint at meaning, without resolving it, why not happily accept it in that state? A harmonious sense, articulable or not, of resolution may (or may not) arise from the poem after it's been tucked in the brain cells for a year or two.

Children can sometimes find themselves in touch with genuine insights particular to the subsurface but equally real self. We may tend to dismiss expressions that lack the trappings of nobility (or even niceness), intellect, and grammar, according to our education, but it would benefit the nurture of the whole human balance of any kid to let the oddest expressive qualities have play, to let poems be unique, like fingerprints, wherever the whorls whirl. The coexistence of such qualities with the standards of good writing is not only possible but healthy and needed, in everyone.

ACROSTICS

Rattles are for babies, but Baby
Always has to
Toy with the
Terribleness of the
Low and partly high
Endless sound.
      —*Shirley Thebaud, 5th*

The playfulness of "babies, but Baby" and the "toy" pun contrast effectively with the spooky characterization of the rattle-sound.

Glory, glory, glory, to God.
His shadows show

Over the haunted house.
Stop
Talking to yourself, I cried.
　　　—Paula Webb, 6th

That he has many shadows, that they hover where they do, links God with
"GHOST." The last two lines seem to indicate that shadows are a form of
speech or that spookiness is introversion and/or that God has a penchant for
creepy mutterings. But to explain links of possible thought in a poem this far
out reduces the sheer startling spiritual surprise; the power of the images and
juxtapositions can be felt better as given. The alliteration and the o's in the
first three lines lend an oratorical splendor to the statement.

Day is like an
Ambush but ambush is not
Yellow. It begins with the sun's
Light. Sunlight is not like an
Influence. It's kind of
Gloomy. It's like when you boil something
Hot. It's so gloomy it looks like garbage mixed with
Thick glue.
　　　—Joseph Iacono, 4th

Light felt as horribly palpable, so much so it's a thing, not an influence. (I too
have had this feeling about it oozing around on things, and have put it in
poems). "Ambush" and "influence" are great words whether or not one can
agreeably share the sensations they evoke.

An acrostic poem is like a
Cool,
Ripe, good-tasting
Orange which is
Simple
To
Imagine that you're
Cutting into slices for yourself.
　　　—Tulio Arroyo, 6th

Once you've divested yourself of the need to mash everything into meaning, by
relaxing and simply enjoying the poem's moves, you may find meaningful connections rising lightly into your mind. An acrostic's construction puts emphasis on
the lines; you can see them as lateral entities like slices. The word "cutting" is
too sharp; perhaps something like "carefully pulling" would work better.

Silver and green
Ugly
But I
Will
Arrange them to
Yellow.
　　　—Wilma Palacios, 5th

Sleight-of-hand underground palette, to imitate the sun.

> Walking away
> On the sky,
> United States
> Lights
> Die.
> —*Doris Marrero, 3rd*

Perhaps the U.S.A. "would" be rash and fly itself away from reality (via imperialism? space probes? hedonism?), and lights die, but the poem's joy is in its combination of original lyric image and brevity.

> Yet
> Everything
> Lies down where people
> Live. They're going
> Overboard and at the
> Wedding they were so happy.
> —*Eddie Garcia, 6th*

The oddity of "yet," as if it followed something (which, we find out, it does—a wedding). A very tough thought on marriage, put in a peculiar dream-like crunch of images. "Everything lies down where people live" is a sophisticated way to speak of routinization. The spine word "YELLOW" is odd too, expressing the fear that may underlie domesticity.

PLACE POEMS

> Connecticut is a place where the streets are smooth. It feels like
> when a shirt was recalled and ironed even more. There are hills
> of grass, the sky as blue as blueberry pie.
> —*Anonymous, 3rd*

The images show the elements of that place to be all tamed, striking a delicate balance that includes that excessive domestication and a genuine niceness.

> I went to the beach and I saw the color green of the grass.
> My mother saw it too and she loved it.
> She stood staring at it.
> Then I bought an ice cream and saw it had the color green.
> And now what can I do?
> My mother may eat my ice cream, o-ma o-ma what can I do?
> I saw a popcorn box and bought it and it was green.
> She tore it out of my hands.
> I called a cop.
> The cop had green eyes.
> I went home and left my mother alone.
> —*Denise Serrano, 4th*

One blade of fantasy (which always begins in the real) grows and takes over the whole scene. "And now what can I do?" is a charm, but the "o-ma o-ma," seeming like a primitive cry, does even more to put the scene into a fabulous perspective. Leaving the mother alone at the end, to eat or be eaten by a world of green, is the right touch. The whole piece, so plainly based in the "real," makes reality seem like a recessive gene.

> The green grass shines.
> Playing in the grass,
> Seeing the gates,
> Swinging on the swing,
> The flowers, the birds,
> Are taking deep breaths.
> The car passes by what it
> Looks like.
> —*Eilibin Zarate, 6th*

A plain natural scene, then suddenly it's all breathing, then all appearance ("what it/Looks like") as the "car passes by." The poem moves from substance to air to illusion—only the moving car is solid at the end—and all done within the terms of a simple little nature poem.

DOMINICAN REPUBLIC

> Its sandy beaches, like hot
> pearls in a cup
> glistening in the yellow sun.
>
> Its waters running in the sand
> like long streams of tinted blue glass...
> —*Rosario Fernandez, 7th*

Two big beautiful metaphors. Each hardens an image, as if to prepare it for storage in memory.

LUNES

> My teeth are
> so white I'm scared to
> take a bite.
> —*Ethel Nimmons, 7th*

Maybe for fear of getting them dirty, but it also has overtones of ominousness, like Moby Dick white, or blinding light.

> I like the
> stars that have a tingle
> with smoky streams.
> —*Dilcia Gonzalez, 4th*

By synesthesia, the stars' visual qualities, as we get them, are changed to something we may feel we are biting into. Stars are so far away that subjective accuracy is unusually different from objective accuracy.

> Ugly singing birds
> stand behind my uncomfortable bed.
> Too much bother.
> —*Ingrid Gonzales, 8th*

In the first two lines, a turnaround of normal bird or bed attractiveness. Last line a big jump in tone, too swift to be heavy-handed, sounding like a throwaway line in a comic routine.

> The sky is
> so blue that it turns
> the other way.
> —*Eric Flowers, 5th*

Somehow we immediately get it that a too-intense blue would, if it didn't want to make us ache, flip over (or cloud itself up).

> The white snow
> shows me that I am
> in balance again.
> —*Joanna Munoz, 5th*

Swift insight, a subtle response perhaps to snow's evenness, which thought can only feebly follow.

> The moon glows
> lonely in the dark street,
> oh oh oh.
> —*Joseph Chang, 6th*

Three moons.

> When a cat
> waves I wave. He lays
> on my grave.
> —*Reinaldo Aguino, 4th*

Ambiguity, kind of a distilled Alfred Noyes piece, with its ghostliness and heavy music.

> Hi, my name
> is Dawn. It's a great
> day to fly.
> —*Dawn Gomez, 4th*

"Dawn" slides into metaphor, from a person to the sky, greased by alliteration and assonance. The "Hi"/"fly" rhyme supports the tone, ties it up.

THING POEMS

> A piano looks very satisfying to me.
> It has white keys that look like teeth.
> It has the pedals that look like feet that you step on.
> It has a brown walnut finish that seems like a lady who can
>   take the pressure of hard times.
>   *—Sharon Watson, 7th*

"Satisfying" sets a nice tone for a piano. Two ordinary but consistent similes follow, and then an absolutely stunning one that makes color/emotion-link an exact science.

> Fire is a big red-hot orange ball spinning in the sky. It is so fast
>   and violent and lights up this galaxy.
> Fire is one big eye staring into yours, and as I dare to glance
>   my eyes start to tear.
> Fire is a current that surrounds you to drown you, if you
>   don't escape.
> Fire is a furious feeling that starts to burn me up inside.
>   *—Susan Mandell, 8th*

Hot energy, each section poised between reality and fantasy. Touches of soundplay move it along, closer and closer and at last inside the person.

> One day when I woke up the sky turned black and purple. When
> I put my clothes on the sky turned green and yellow. When I put
> my shoes on the sky turned peach and brown. Then when I
> washed my mouth the sky turned red and violet. When I ate
> cornflakes the sky finally turned blue.
>   *—Lizbeth Diaz, 2nd*

> When I open an egg
> I see an embryo,
> and sometimes I put eggs
> under my bed for tomorrow
> for lunch.
> And when I take the eggs out
> I see chicks cracking out
> of them.
> Everytime I look at the chicks
> they grow mustaches.
> Everytime I look at the egg
> it looks like the Empire State Building.
>   *—David Vigo, 2nd*

Two second-graders dancing off reality. Lizbeth's poem puts fantasy beautifully in service of a system. Note how the word "finally" humanizes the feel of the poem. David follows random but true-to-mind jumps, accelerating.

"REAL-LIFE" PIECES

when the light hit the
sun it shine as a golden
egg. yesterday was the
sixteenth day of my life.
you make me feel happy
across the moon. when you light
up my life I hate it.
the woodpecker is almost
as ugly as (blank).
Mickey Mouse is good as count-
ing like my grandaunt 6 - 10 - 5 - 2 - 1.
it's uncount aunt. the minute
I stepped outside I turned
into Mary Poppin.
—*Vielka Atkins, 6th*

Various *types* of off-ness, a little shaky at first but she's cooking by the end.

When I played chess with my big brother, I felt that I could win.
Then we started to play. We had 1 1/2 hours playing. I looked at
the chessboard and the squares. The players were him and me,
alone in the living-room. I still felt I could win. The squares
looked like cages where there were lots of dogs inside telling me
where to move in the game. I won my brother, but I felt I cheated,
so next time I will play with my mind, not with imagination.
—*Rafael Torres, 7th*

A sober drama, of the sort wherein the hero stubbornly passes up the Star of India despite the most obvious pressures. And maybe he's right to.

THE ACCIDENT

One blazing afternoon I felt real happy. I thought maybe I should
try eating liver for a change. I took a walk with my family down
a flaming rainbow. When suddenly a big blue station wagon
went swift over my body. From that minute on I saw black air
filling my eyes until I was conscious again. I saw people in white
surrounding me.
—*Anthony Fraticelli, 6th*

Humor and tragedy take turns but at last are eclipsed by power of vision: "I saw black air filling my eyes."

Once I saw a cat. It went by and a hair fell. I saw the black hair. It
was tiny. It was soft. I kept staring at it. I thought I was in a pile
of nice soft black fur. The cat came back, looked at me and left. It
left me alone with the little black hair. All by myself.
—*Anthony, 3rd*

As if the world in a grain of sand were made of sand. The cat is mysterious, semi-absent, as cats are. Aloneness comes when you're back where you started. A poignant piece.

> I woke up and I looked at my ceiling. I saw all kinds of shapes and colors. It looked like a man calling names at somebody else and people running to see what is what, and it started to rain. Then I woke up and I looked at my window and it started to rain.
> —Lana Larsen, 5th

First the wakeup, then the dream quality of awakeness emerges, as shapes in the ceiling proceed from image to story. Then the second wakeup stage, and the dream is physically carried over, ceiling to window. Now it's outside. Whew.

> I went to visit my cousin who lived in the twelfth floor that had white windows like the shining hot sun. I went in the elevator. It had small square rainbow colorful plates on the floor. In the red and white colorful walls it seemed that it held the air that will lift you up. The white lights up in the ceiling that looked like white birds shined the walls like the heavy sun that is near the earth.
> —Richard De La Rosa, 5th

No doubt about it, though the innocence (or ignorance) of correct language would eventually merely limit this poet, right now it helps him avoid certain traps (such as glibness) and achieve a quick touch of heaven.

> She was so sad that she laughed all the way home.
> Because she felt like eating herself.
> But she did not eat herself.
> She ate paper and then she ate birds.
> And she ate some more paper and birds.
> At last somebody came and they hit her because she ate birds
>   and paper.
> When they hit her she did not cry.
> She laughed until it rained.
> —Joanne Liriano, 3rd

The last laugh goes to the spirit world. Joanne turns things upside down in various ways.

> I was walking in the street and I saw a dog with orange spots. I was startled and told my mother. I wore a skirt so long that it reached my ankles. I was heading east and it seemed like a plane and truck started to follow me. Then they were coming towards me, but they missed. The sky started to thunder but it was only the crash of the white plane and black truck. The dog that I saw was barking as loud as the crash.
> —Luz Marin, 6th

Complications. The most "meaningful" event seems to be the crash of black and white, as if those colorless, aggressive extremes were, happily, knocking each other off. That the colorful dog is barking "as loud" exerts different pulls. "Long skirt," "east" seem loaded to bear meaning, too, but what? Memorability in a poem may be defined as an enduring balance between meaning and something else, tipping neither way.

Chapter XIII

CONCISION, SHAPELINESS, AND UNDERSTATEMENT

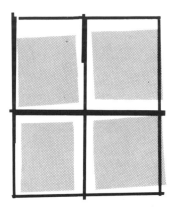

"I had a/ star in my eye and/ came out fast"

Concision is a famous virtue of good poetry, including *The Odyssey* and the "wordy" works of Gertrude Stein. Concision is not the same as brevity, though it contains it. I take concision to mean a process rather than a result, saying things in small compass, though the whole thing said may be long or manifold. And what does "saying things" mean exactly in poetry? It is not merely the paraphrasable content but also all the tones and felt connotations that make poetry poetry. So concision doesn't mean a paring-down to denotation. Poetic concision produces an impacted sense of energy, however smoothly the words flow.

One result of concision, beyond the efficiency of it, is the "jam effect." Words, images, phrases may have new meanings revealed when they are packed in closely with other words, images, and phrases. Emotions can be intensified. The rapidity of thought-change can resemble actual mind-workings; as Allen Ginsberg remarked, "Mind is shapely."

By shapeliness I mean chiefly an experimental trust in one's inherent sense of form, expressing itself in appropriate line-lengths, original syntax speeding things up or slowing them down as needed, giving organic rather than artificially structured emphases. Sometimes multiple threads can be woven, giving a feeling of dimension to the poem's linearity. A baroque tension can be achieved when pauses in the poem only half-conceal ongoing currents. A sense of dichotomy is often played with by "slanting" against proposals rather than opposing them directly.

Understatement ain't much.

ACROSTICS

> I don't know.
> Take it away.
> —*Dana Ring, 8th*

Concise to get outa there quick.

> Large
> Income
> Brings
> Rage
> Around the head.
> —*Nelson Chin, 7th*

Concise, and also the verb in the middle exemplifies the balance point of Libra.
The rage is made expressive by the longer last line.

> Great Adventure
> Or Disneyland,
> Or maybe you can
> Do something at home.
> —*Veronica Franklin, 6th*

> Some day, some
> Time,
> Around the
> Room I dance.
> —*Vanessa Velasquez, 3rd*

> Little
> Olive,
> Roll
> Down.
> —*Lucy Torres, 3rd*

In each case, sudden shifts between large and small, spine word to message.

> How did you do
> It? It is a good song for a short
> Time.
> —*William Rodriguez, 4th*

A perfect hit.

> Happy means
> A lot of
> Pears falling off a
> Pear tree and
> You pick up the pears and make a pie.
> —*Linda Romano, 5th*

Serendipity in the short lines, but labor in a long line.

> A dog was
> Lost and I
> Said,
> "Okay—another dog."
> —*Rosa Medina, 3rd*

Everything around me
Now is
Just so full
Of
You and me.
—*Joseph Caracciola, 3rd*

Little structures of toughness and love, respectively. The "me" in the first line of Joseph's poem would be more harmonious as "us," but maybe what's expressed is more accurate; none of us can really speak for another, no matter how close.

Growing up is hard.
It means to cry and cry.
Rafe doesn't like me, and I don't
Like him either.
—*Zoila Blanco, 8th*

What's good about this poem is the sudden change from pallid generality to pungent realism, as if the generality were giving birth. "GIRL" seems defined within a sense of tragedy. Last line-break sets things up well.

Fire is an
Incredible friend
Ready to turn into an incredible
Enemy.
—*Santiago Negron, 6th*

Different line-placings of "incredible" swing to the turn of meaning.

Closed is
Like blocking
Off
Something that might be
Excellent, or maybe it's just a plain
Door.
—*Jose Garcia, 6th*

Line length here delineates a shapely double shutting — the slow "Off" prefiguring the final "Door."

Oh yes, I'm nice, I'm kind, I'm
Socialized. I have the touch of
Classification. I got as much class
As the whole nation. I'm the one and only Master
Rock.
—*Oscar Castro, 5th*

Feverish streetspeed and rhyme lead up to solid "Rock."

Spray me off.
Peel out

In a whiz.
Now I'm dizzy.
　　　　—*Phillip Tockman, 5th*

Whizbang.

Alphabet of names and faces,
Ugly and beautiful.
Names you can't remember.
Terrific people who can
Stand you.
　　　　—*Denise Smith, 6th*

Beautiful first line. Sensible insights throughout, ending in "stand you" alone, emphasized, even ultimate, reminding one that home is where they have to let you in.

Keep
On
Using
The
Right
Of
Speech.
　　　　—*Thomas Koutros, 6th*

What perfect slogan had his name been Williamson or Wojciehowicz?

Money is something everybody
On this world wants.
Nobody that I know doesn't like money,
Even
You.
　　　　—*Angelina Cinco, 6th*

Girls are nice
In
Rooms
Like
Stars are nice in the sky.
　　　　—*Cathalina S., 3rd*

Opposite extreme uses of line length, each appropriate, each drawing power to the ending.

Daylight
Around us.
When?
Now.
　　　　—*Dawn Mace, 5th*

Sun pops up like a cosmic piece of toast.

> The day
> Is going by and
> My mother comes home in the
> Evening.
> —*Elizabeth C., 5th*

Poignancy from a minimum, almost an absence, of material.

> Some people are sad
> And others are
> Dead.
> —*Sean H., 4th*

> Love your mother
> Or your father. Take a
> Vow and say, "I do." Have a kid.
> End the whole thing.
> —*Michelle, 5th*

Different styles of quickness in the two poems. The first resembles water going down a drain, the second a leaping brook.

> Have
> Always
> Pride in what
> People
> Yell at you for.
> —*Sojourna Thompson, 6th*

Shapely defiance. "Always" is properly emphasized by standing alone. The rhythm—lines 2 and 4 versus lines 3 and 5—is nice. The order in which the elements arise is dramatically sound; the last line has punch.

PLACE POEM

DISNEYLAND

> What a place to be,
> Mickey Mouse and me.
> —*Laura Kaplan, 5th*

Such a conglomerate of giantism as Disneyland is the right place for extreme concision.

LUNES

> The rain falls
> on top of everybody, but
> not on me.
> —*Wanda Santiago Julia, 7th*

Lune shape flawlessly used. The long second line is made even longer by the multi-syllabled "everybody," which emphasizes the swift surprise in the last line.

> Go to Heaven.
> If it's nice, call me.
> I'll be there.
> —*Jennifer Leyden, 3rd*

Note how much faster the last line is than the first. The poem comes to life nicely by taking on, step by step, the quickness of everyday speech.

> I had a
> star in my eye and
> came out fast.
> —*Robert Rivera, 3rd*

Appropriate jam of ideal (line 2) and hip (line 3). The Sugar Ray Story.

> The summer is
> hot and I like it
> because, the pool.
> —*Corinne Madera, 5th*

Delicious rescue from dullness in the ", the pool."

> I thought it
> so, but now I know
> better than to.
> &
> Spring is time
> for me to blossom out
> of my shell.
> &
> Life is short
> so we have to squeeze
> everything in it.
> &
> The rockets blast.
> The ships sail, but I
> just sit here.
> &
> Sun is hot,
> wind is fierce, but I
> am strong too.
> —*Anna Depalo, 5th*

Taken each by itself, the middle three lunes are too derivative, but they are elements in a series I find to be a touching self-portrait.

> My little mother
> walks down the sidewalk with
> a plastic bag.
> —*Angela Hayes, 3rd*

Beautifully noncommital. "Little" charms without sentimentality.

> A book is
> big, a book is small.
> Maybe that's all.
> —*Layonta, 4th*

Seems to say, with effortless brevity and rhyme, that "maybe" physical facts are the ultimate facts.

> What happened to
> me and not to you
> can be words.
> —*Jeanette Orsini, 5th*

Origin of speech made simple.

> Who makes food?
> I don't know. Ask adults.
> They might know.
> —*Maria Saona, 3rd*

Understatement so far under (line 3) that it's funny. But, then again, do we really know the answer?

> If you like
> gum then go buy it
> and chew it.
> —*Anonymous, 3rd*

Spareness, especially last line, exposes the skull-like look of extreme gum-chewing. Also, there's a mastication sound in "buy it/ and chew it."

WILLIAM CARLOS WILLIAMS IMITATIONS

> I'm so sorry I looked at your diary,
> but I was desperate to find what
> was in it. So I didn't like it.
> So I put lipstick on it. It
> was funny then.
> —*Nichola Tucker, 4th*

Good slapstick joke. The changing tone of the "so's" moves the overall tone from apologetic to brazen.

> Sorry to say
> I exploded your house
> but it looked so
> nice up in the
> air. But I don't
> think your cat

> and dog liked it when they went
> and never came back.
> —*Adolphus Reid, 4th*

Extreme. Deadpan. The combination of "when" and "never" in the last part is funny, whether intentional or just a natural turn of language.

> I'm sorry that I put the baby
> in the bathtub, but I thought she could
> swim.
> —*Anonymous, 4th*

Understatement. That she *couldn't* swim is never said.

> This is just to say
> Sorry for embarassing
> you at the dance when I poured spaghetti
> on your white dress but it was
> kind of interesting looking at you
> while you were screaming at me
> for doing that.
> —*Angela Knight, 6th*

That these are imitations helps the students, for one thing, paradoxically, work out their own sense of line lengths, the Williams poem being clearly, constantly broken up in the middle of things. Here "kind of" and the way "for doing that" is isolated at the very end are very funny delicacies of language. The poem seems to climax in line 5 and then to twist tighter yet into the last two.

> This is just to say
> I'm sorry I read your diary,
> but you read mine last week.
> You can make a new one
> that I didn't read.
> —*Melinda Joy Nixon, 1st*

Solemnly illogical (that being able to create *more* privacy could make up for privacy being invaded), all the funnier.

VARIOUS POEMS

> Your life is nice, your life is sweet.
> Don't lose it on 103rd Street...
> —*Noel Velazquez, 8th*

Rhythm lives within concision.

> Momma, Momma, don't cry, I am jumping
> in the blue sky.
> —*Anthony Fraser, 4th*

Likewise.

ABOUT POETRY

> Poetry is like
> a movie star
> with no fans.
> —*April Chin, 6th*

How did she know that?

> Poetry is like thinking of nothing when you know what to
> think of.
> —*Anthony Ferrari, 5th*

A zenlike statement about openness.

> Poetry is like the dirt rushing in your face.
> —*Randy, 6th*

"Dirt rushing" is an unusual image. It can be taken as an affirmation of poetry's reality.

> Poetry's like seeing something that makes you feel like you've
> seen it before.
> —*Tamiko Griffin, 6th*

The sense of familiarity creates a field for mentally joining one thing to another.

> Poetry is like standing under a rainstorm and letting your nose
> run without caring.
> —*Tonyi Korona, 6th*

Yes, one feels more alone, though more connected, in the water.

> Poetry is like a cloud. It rains when it wants to.
> —*Orlando Crespo, 6th*

The unpredictability of inspiration.

> Poetry is a
> slow flash
> of light
> because it comes
> to you piece by
> piece.
> —*Felix Rivera, 6th*

The exact role of words in regard to spirit is shown. Waves change to particles in this poem. That is, words, by their nature, metamorphose the light-wave-like flashes of poetic insight to fragmented forms. We may change these particles back to wave form in our minds when we read/hear a poem. As with movies, a flow is put into static, interrupted bits and reassembled mentally to flow. Thus the paradox of the "slow flash" holds.

   This poem well illustrates the powers of concision. "Poetry is a slow flash of light because it comes to you" is as economical as a dictionary definition, each word a bare necessity of the meaning. Thus there's a feeling of an energy held in. Then a relative opening out of the grammar in "piece by/piece" (he could have said "in pieces" or "fragmentarily"), harmonious with the breaking-up sense it denotes.

Chapter XIV

ADULTNESS

"A sort of dangerous associated system I love"

In various ways, the poems of children will sometimes be notably affected by adult or adult-like thought and feeling. Sustainable skill with words, with verse forms and the structuring of free verse, and with consistency of ideas, all help us write well. What one often sees in schoolchildren, though, is a decrease in poetic impact as these skills are assimilated. The very word "skill" seems to connote a mechanical response.

It's true that some kids are able to mix a retained child-sensibility with their increased expressive skills, but most aren't. It's a process in which they have no guides, usually, and usually lack the philosophic fineness to juggle successfully their growing perspective and their energy. Good adult poetry is often unavailable to them — either it just plain doesn't come into their ken or its language refinements and sophisticated points of reference make it unrecognizable to them. The culture at large — wherein poetry is seen, unfortunately, as highly specialized — gives the child little with which to combat such influences.

It is difficult to know how poetry may survive personally for even a very receptive child. Some combination of care and criticism tempered with honoring the kid's own vision, however "wrong" it may seem — benign neglect perhaps — can help keep the spark alive, through the heaves and confusions of growing up. Simply presenting inclined kids with good poetry and letting them ride it as they will may be best for some; assignments may work well for others. Reading aloud, concentrating on the visceral, leaving one's "philosophy" out of it, is likely to let the magic flourish and stick.

ACROSTICS

Wedding in the skies
Ending overnight.

Dreams are just dreams.
Doing this job in fright.
In the morning skies
Nothing will be happening.
Going, going, gone.
—*Maria Camargo, 5th*

Beautiful poem, heart breaking sophistication. The first two lines expand and deflate the wedding quickly. Next, the dream is cut to basics. Next, zilch. And in the last line the disappearance is snappily recapitulated. Good use of a cliché.

Spell
Pestacide.
Excellent.
Let's now spell
Lunitic.
Impossable!
Now spell quiz.
Good work.
—*Fayola Goode, 5th*

Adult-like playfulness (from a base of superior knowledge).

Departing from the
Elemental plane of the Earth,
Always
Trying to return to the
Human state.
—*Jamal Rodgers, 6th*

Bright boy piles up vocabulary and good thought, making death seem anxious rather than restful. "State" vs. "plane" is food for thought. But some image or concreteness would give the piece vividness.

Why does it always have to
Happen to me?
Year after year
My life fades away into
Eternity.
God, please give me hope to carry
On with my life.
Dear God, why me?
—*Leslie Santiago, 6th*

Hot choice of backbone words. There's an air of "literary" skill about the poem, which partially blurs (being clichéd) and partially enables (being articulate) the poetic focus, the attempt to pull the personal out of the universal.

LUNES

Las aves vuelan,
vuelan alto por las nubes
que bellas lucen.
—Damaris Mora, 5th

("The birds fly/ they fly high through the clouds/ that shine beautifully").
Pretty.

The old man's
heart was just not what
I had expected.
—Kyle Owens, 5th

Strangely focused on the impossibility of knowing another's heart. Expectations frankly adult. Sense of ambivalence between the physical and emotional
meanings of "heart."

WILLIAM CARLOS WILLIAMS IMITATION

THIS IS JUST TO SAY

I have given
your favorite geraniums
to the dog
for dinner.
The order in
which she ate
them was fascinating.
Slowly disappearing
into an opening
and closing door.
—Naomi Berner, 5th

Adult-like language skill (especially in line-breaks) refines the surreal.

VARIOUS POEMS

THAT HOUSE

What happens in that house
after dusk falls
that makes the whole town shiver?

What happens in that house
with the gray and black shutters
and shingles that flap in the night?

138

What happens in that house
where doors are always creaking
and where creatures look for someone to bite?

What happens in that house?
Well, nobody knows.
They don't dare go in.
　　　　—Hazel, 8th

Chant. Skill in "poetic" language again accompanied by predictability in both syntax and concept.

I like to comb my hair.
I comb it every day.
Day after day I comb my hair.
I chew gum while I comb my hair.
I comb my hair all day long.
My hair is curly; when I wash it it turns straight.
I comb my hair while birds are singing.
　　　　—Catalina Curbelo, 6th

I was sitting in my room
listening to rock music,
thinking about the past and future
and what will become of us.

I was looking out the window
on a nice Spring day, watching
the birds go by very swiftly.
　　　　—Jean McGuire, 6th

These two pick up on book-learned poeticisms, chiefly the introduction of birds when a lyric climax is too obviously wanted. Nice, but a stage to get through for poet and non-poet.

THIN SNOW

soft white snow covering the earth's surface
like grinding coconuts from the sky to Earth
like creating joy from an infant's birth
floating around spitting white snow
floating around the snow brings joy
around the earth like a toy
landing with a soft sound around the earth
falling down softly swishing all through the air
without a bump lying down softly with no crash
　　　　—Sonia Polanco, 5th

A mixture of poetic gift and the lack of confidence (almost universal as a developmental stage) that makes one copy tones of language.

WOMAN/CHILD

As I sit on my veranda swing
    as I sit on the playground swing
watching my birds fly about
    watching some pigeons take off
my lover alights from his horse
    Tony gets off his bike
how he showed his love for me
    how he gave me a sweetheart candy
I think he loves me.
    I bet he likes me.
       —*Denise Smith, 6th*

Obvious focus on form doesn't detract from vivacity. On the contrary, Denise has the confidence that lets her be both child and adult.

As I sit down drinking tea
    as hot as first love
I think about outer space and what lies ahead.
Viciously the Milky Way glows.
Brilliantly do the stars mix red, blue and white.
The sun seems yellow but really is a white star.
Now while I'm thinking, my tea is
as cold as ice.
       —*Collette Neils, 6th*

Adult skill need not suffocate child life. Strife of the two dissolves into the content.

OVER THE BLUE MOUNTAINS

The sun is rising in the east over the blue mountains,
lighting up the dark black sky into a blue garden.
The birds sing and flap their wings in their awakening.
The earth is warmed, a seed grows into a red rose.
The city noise begins to shout as people start coming out.
Children cry and cats meow as they are awakened.
A new day has started in our land,
Over the blue mountains
Over the blue mountains.
       —*Edward Crespo, 7th*

Second (blue garden) line is lovely. Speed of rose's growth gives the piece a feeling of universality. Then, when the "new day" has fallen off in energy, the last two lines return a lyric sense.

echoes in a cave,
echoes in the mind
sounding sounding again.

church bells in the belfry,
horns of a car,

sounding sounding again.

whispers of the wind
whispers in the wind

sounding sounding
again.

joyful laughter in the air
mournful cries in the air

sounding sounding
again.
            —*Edward Crespo, 7th*

Here the same poet has gone farther, but unfortunately into poetic cliché. Such changes as "of" to "in" in the two whispers lines are evidence of a real care for details of thought, but the emphasis lies in an a priori, thus cloudy, sense of poetic beauty, whose tired generalities are made to create a knee-jerk lofty atmosphere.

> At night I sit down on the side of my bed wondering while the cold and icy wondrous stars of the night are out. I wonder, awaiting what lies ahead for me the next day. I could be devoured by a pack of mad dogs or gunned down by hoodlums. I might have frostbite because of the icy day that takes all of the warmth out of my body. In my Chemistry class I might develop a new serum to stop any kind of Cancer. Suddenly my eyes close, I lie down and it is calm and warm as the moon brilliant and observing light.
>   —*Collette Neils, 6th*

This is cast in a mode of thought ripely romantic, reaching with her brightness a few years ahead to the type of derivative individualism rife, unfortunately, among teenagers. However, the poet's verve is not quashed, a word like "observing" helps save it, and the very broadness of the treatment, confounding any too-dry critical sense, seems to express the bright girl more than just the style she's working in.

> I remember when I broke a plate, in the kitchen. As the plate was falling I was scared and very mad at myself. I went to the closet and got the broom and the dust-pan and cleaned it up. When my mother came home, I told her what happened and started to cry. My mother said that she's not mad, and accidents do happen. I told her I'd be more careful next time. She said "O.K." I don't really know how she feels.
>   —*Kelley Harrison, 5th*

A very adult, in the best sense, approach to phenomena of daily life, adamantly resistant to the sentiment of the moment and without the need to show off. In other words, the careful phrasing of the bulk of the piece creates a mood of tolerance, overcoming the wild stuff that lies behind everything. Then, just as we are convinced of this, the poem is opened up again, in the last sentence, not with any overemotional high color like "she was probably shaking inside with frustration," however, rather with a minimal but unrestrictive expression.

"REAL-LIFE" PIECES

EX DRAGON FIGHTER

I would kill the fire-breathing dragon with my laser beam sword
and my reflected shield. I was a hero in the town of Maple Berry.
But those days are over. Now all I do is fix shoes. Sometimes
when I hit a shoe with a hammer, I remember when the sky
turned dark, when I would kill the green creature. Those days
were the golden days. Now these are the silver days.
     —Anthony Pereira, 5th

A clear portrayal of "used-to-be." Special charms are the name "Maple Berry," the economy of such wordage as "Now all I do is fix shoes," the causal connection between hitting the shoe with a hammer and the sky turning dark, "the green creature" (a hint at universality, as if it stood for all the evil in his life), and the fine rue of "golden" and "silver."

My friend and I went hiking one day.
We sat under a tree
and let our thoughts just slip away.
We thought of movies, clothes and boys,
because honestly I think we're too old to play
with toys.
We sat there in a daze,
my mind in a maze,
making rights, making lefts,
reaching all sorts of depths.
Then we rose to our feet
and walked slowly to meet
reality.
     —Leslie Santiago, 6th

Emphasis is so much of a poem's essence, and emphasis is so much determined by nuances of language tone, a very natural matter in turn determined by personality and how one feels about one's relation with language and life. Here the embracing of academic skills both helps and hinders the poem. In detail, the expressivity is too smooth (the iambics of lines 3 and 4, "reaching...depths," "meet reality"), but the whole picture contains a salubrious self-deprecation (the humorous tone of "making rights, making lefts"), a realistic grain—perhaps midwifed by Hispanic big-city life — that vitiates the vague earnestness of much of the poetry by youngsters successful in school.

I was walking along a bridge when suddenly I saw a little fish
peeking at me from behind a cloud. I ignored it. But I couldn't help

looking back at it. Finally I got so angry I reached out and grabbed the fish. As I did this, the white sky fell on me. I was terrified. I didn't know what to do. Gasping, choking sounds came from my mouth. I tried to speak. I couldn't. My voice was gone. My voice, along with all my senses. What were they doing to me? They were swallowing me alive. Then suddenly the nosy little fish came and lifted the sun into its rightful place, and we walked off into the sunset.

    —*Leslie Santiago, 6th*

Another piece by the same person. The imagination seems mostly caught in a cutesy series more literarily than personally inspired. A piece like this may make a teacher feel fine, combining the successes of English teaching with a harmless dreamlike play, but the spiritual values in poetry require the teacher's willingness to approve thrusts not only apart from but even contrary to the necessary instructional standards. The struggle in poetry is to master *and* transcend standards, to catch the personal response within us, inventing, if not a language, a tone, as we go. The advantage and disadvantage of children is their lesser mastery. Thus the frequent serendipity of ignorance, which can't last. Leslie's prose poem is fine but not inspired.

Late at night I look up in the sky,
there are billions of stars but just one caught my eye.
It was the smallest but shiny like day.
It twinkled as if it was laughing
as it moved across the sky, laughing and giggling
as if it was at a party. The next day I
woke up and rushed to the window
and it was gone.

    —*Curtis, 8th*

Here a sincere feeling, desire for that one special thing, is co-opted into a cliché by the slight shift into standardized symbols, beginning in line 3.

Walking in the wilderness one day, I was singing as I was skip-ping and someone else sings along. I look around everywhere and I see the robin that was singing with me. We become pals and walk along in the quiet wilderness. And to my surprise, who or what do I see? The bear that was following me. I ran as fast as I could. Robin got scared and flew away. I finally lost the bear. Robin came back. And then to my second surprise, who or what do I see? The big bad wolf that was glad when he saw us. For din-ner I would be, and dessert robin. But we escaped and became free. At last I could have some fun alone, only me and robin and me and robin forever. And ever me and robin forever and ever together.

    —*Maria Perdikis, 4th*

I love her quick robin dessert, and the last lyric cry. Narrative with child-like (personal particular) jumps and oddities unsullied. The impact of primitive art.

> The blueblack glob
> came towards me
> and
> I hid in an attaché case
> and
> jumped to Queens
> and
> the graduating class practiced on my aunt's porch
> and
> my class sang
> and
> danced to wild music from an elevator
> and
> I got off
> and...
> woke up.
>> —*Denise Smith, 6th*

Despite the heavy use of formal elements (such as the "and" routine) and the adult-like skill, the emphasis here (until the end, which is uninspired, the old Wizard-of-Oz dream washaway) remains in Denise's imaginative qualities. She doesn't get stuck in the form.

ABOUT POETRY

> When you open the door
> of your mind,
> poetry slips in.
> You don't know what to do,
> so you knock on your mind's door.
> Then you think maybe poetry is poor;
> it does not have a home of its own
> to live in.
> Maybe poetry is a dinosaur;
> maybe it is a small
> dinosaur and will turn into
> a big one and blow my mind.
> Ahhh, poetry, get out or else!
> And I lay dead—too bad.
> Boooo hoooo, good-bye everybody.
> Poetry has killed me. You poetry
> ghost, I will get you—soon you
> will be sorry, you poetry ghost.
> You will be sorry.
> My ghost shall
> get you.
> Ohhoohhh, I hate you!
> And so I got the poetry

ghost and killed him—my ghost never saw him again.
I lived in peace after that.
You will also when you kill
a poetry ghost.
Growl, goes the ghost, Nay nay,
you can't
catch me—I caught him!
Boo hoo, he said—you're too fast.
I will get you—you will be
sorry, you person ghost. I will
get you, he said. *I will get you,*
I said back. So I got him
and ate him up. Good-bye, poetry ghost.
   —*Moona Saima, 4th*

An amazing myth-like narrative of a struggle with poetry, in which poetry loses in the story but wins in the fact of the poem's existence. The apparent confusions are simply unrationalized elements of struggle, which have their organic shapes, the repetition of the triumph, the casting of poetry as villain. At last he's eaten up, absorbed within in a more viable manner. The presumption of future use is unsaid but you are what you eat and what else could enliven that triumphant "peace"?

My life is a poem. I love my little poems, tiny words shattered in a sort of system in my heart, in a sort of little voice, could be to me. A poem is like little suns in my face when I shatter the words that appear in mind that I put in a sort of dangerous associated system I love.

Poems should be positive and strong, raising and raising. When words appear in a system it could be positive or an accident or nature sorting it to life, if you put it that way.
   —*Melissa Kawecky, 3rd*

Where this came from God only knows. Maybe, in part, from the dictionary as far as sheer vocabulary ("dangerous associated system") goes. She may have just learned "shatter" and "system," and "a sort" of beginner's luck has perhaps attended her use of them, but there it is. "Tiny words shattered in a sort of system in my heart, in a sort of little voice" would honor Keats, or anyone speaking of poetry. "Raising and raising" shows the tell of "positive and strong." And the three things "it could be," when words "appear" in a system: positive/accident/nature sorting it to life, "put it that way" that divides without dividing, like a trinity can be.

Poem like an unknown
world
How would it begin
or how
would it end it's
just

145

something of a feeling
that walks
into your mind it
controls
the mind for you
to write
about it difficult
it is not
to know a poem
'cause a
poem makes you
realize
what or how you
feel inside
about anything
to be
wrong or to be
right it
doesn't matter
all you
have to do is
float with the sky
and the feelings.
    —Sandra Peralta, 8th

Formal line-breaks, rhythm, and lack of punctuation make up for predictability
(as in "makes you/realize/what or how you/feel inside"), by helping direct attention to the exemplifying dance.

Chapter XV

EMPATHY

"Like I was whirling around in the sky"

Empathy, a sense of identification with someone or something outside one's self, is strongly present in and behind nearly all the poems
in this book, or in any good book of poems.
Beyond such exercises as "I am a floor; people are always stepping on me," empathy is
perhaps the basic movement of emotion from which poetry springs. The "I am
the floor" type of expression, in fact, tends to miss true empathy. It anthropo-
morphizes, usually in derivative ways. Rather than feeling from another
thing's standpoint, it transfers known feelings to a mask of that thing. The
mental effort requires simply recalling what people say. To really project an
open readiness to feel one's way into a situation apart from the self, beyond
the clichés of sympathy, is a matter of much focused effort and/or inspiration.

To speak of empathy, we must first think about perception. To think of
perception, we must consider the cluster of impulses that motivates us to
register things not so much as they are but as we need them to be. The
philosopher Husserl and others have shown us clearly how much distortion at-
tends all of our perceptions. Tremendous physical and psychological factors in-
ject a lot of subjectivity into our understanding of everything we take in. One
witness sees two culprits in a red getaway car, another sees three in a blue
van. The lawns we see as green and smooth are mixed rainbows of reflection
and jungles of texture. The person we quickly label according to our needs
would take libraries to but half explain. A smile is a baring of fangs and vice
versa. A spiral takes us in, out, or nowhere.

This, however, does not merely constitute barriers in the path to perception.
The electron microscope is not the acme of aesthetic focus. The limits and
distortions of our perception are in themselves fodder and structure for our
art. The human condition is achingly true in its average delicacies, not just in
its extremes. We live in surfaces, cultural nuances, crosscurrents, and all kinds
of styles.

Perception varies. There are as many ways of seeing things as there are individuals on earth, and this can be multiplied by the various minutes in the life of each. There is no absolute right or wrong about it; the various perceptions constitute a spectrum of availability to humanity at large.

In other words, empathy is always "imperfect." All the focused efforts in the world will not make us truly objective. Out of the necessary mixture of self and sense, however, style emerges. In great literature, the degree in which a sense of self seems to infuse the style ranges from Blake, in whose writings it is very strong, to Shakespeare, whose own viewpoint seems absent from the work. Blake saw everything in terms of his personal angels; Shakespeare let his characters be themselves (except they all loved language). Mark Twain wrote with a strong sense of self, but this does not mean that his perception was correspondingly dimmed. On the contrary, it seems to have been heightened by his expansiveness. The matter is much more complex than a simple dichotomy. Empathy need not be whole and direct to function well. It can be based on such slant or surface perceptions as those of manners, material goods, and speech patterns and still be expressive of what lies behind them.

The empathy of children tends to be undeveloped, to exist in flashes. It can be breathtakingly keen. When the candidness of a child lights on something outside the self, empathy is there in its pure form, if only for a moment. The exercise of poetry can help develop empathy in kids to a surprising degree, because empathy is sustained by writing down instances of it.

Empathy, however, cannot be imposed; it must be tickled out. It cannot be so much taught as invited. But learning has always depended as much on its allure as on its routine. Then, when children are writing, struggling to pay attention to something (which is a lot of what empathy is), the empathy of the teacher comes into play. We as teachers cannot be confident that we will easily recognize *their* empathy. It takes a mighty transcending of oneself (including one's ideas about what is right) to be alert to the perceptions that may lie under the often unskilled language of kids. In the case of creative writing the soul of "what is right" is the individual perception. This should be sought out and encouraged. When hostility is involved in the perception (see Aaron's poems, pp. 61-63), there are considerations to balance. No one principle will cover. Outright quashing could cause the hostility to fester or to express itself in more harmful ways than writing. But an uncritical tolerance doesn't help the kid do more than blow off steam. When some steam is off, a channeling of subject matter, or challenges of compositional form, can help expand the kid's attention to things outside his personal frustrations.

Individual perception takes place in syntax as well as subject matter. That is, the language kids choose may be part of their vision. Thus, case-by-case decisions, rather than blanket application of principles, are appropriate, even when grammar is incorrect.

If empathy is, among other things, a sort of medicine, then preventive empathy can be practiced in teaching writing. Poetry seems so optional that a lot depends on the mood that has been developed in class concerning the worth of the whole enterprise. When I first conducted writing workshops I made the mistake of overemphasizing the polemics of my own fervent belief that art is great. Such soapbox tactics both alienate and bore students. I found that, for me, such a degree of flung challenge is not the fruitful atmosphere. It doesn't even represent what I cherish, because it's too abstract.

Work seems to teach me that everyone, especially when young, has a poten-tiality for poetry. The barriers in the way of its true expression are strong. They stand mainly in protective attitudes that grow from normal civilized self-interest — it's hard to, as it were, take a deep breath and be genuinely vulnerable. But part of the vision of poetry involves going beyond such reluc-tance. The best way past these barriers is not over them or through them but around them—by taking a path relatively free of them: direct experience. Ra-tional discussion can help fix in mind—but can never substitute for—the in-sights gained by emotional experience. What leads on best for me is jumping right into poetry in terms the students don't have to translate. Getting them to write is as appropriate in poetry as is practice—as opposed to thought alone —in music; and giving lively examples, often of kids' work, is crucial. There is no sense in attempting to force them to love what you love, trying to "explain" them into the joys of "A Valediction Forbidding Mourning" through walls of alien phraseology and referential scope. On the other hand, one should never use, as a means of catalyzing their enthusiasm, a poem one doesn't seriously like. And they *should* be given adult poems; the consistency available there is not usually maintained in children's work. There is good poetry, especially near-contemporary, in which the *tone of the language* is not off-putting to kids. Finding such works may require some research on the part of the teacher, since even a "good" education may lag decades behind in poetry.

The personality of the teacher and/or poet cannot be scanted as a means of making poetry come alive. This doesn't mean taking time off, even for a minute, to become palsy-walsy; for the visiting poet it means letting one's per-sonality *as poet* emerge in a natural way and hoping that the connection be-tween that image and the images kids already relate to becomes valid to them. One gets one's poetic licks in—the statements that will help students see the way—when opportunity arises, not through the sole force of having the floor.

It's not necessarily easy, as a school hireling, to bring a classful of perhaps bored, rebellious, pragmatic, puberty-obsessed, intellectually passive, materialism-ridden, self-interest-keyed people, with the attention span of a flashbulb and with a ready contempt for the impracticality, goofiness, and "ef-feminacy" of the poetic impulse, to the point where they can applaud and eagerly create something that challenges all their "faults," something in which the riskiness of violating standards is a prime virtue. Kids, in their vulnerabili-ty, depend on standards. But the approval is inside them. Via personal believability and their own powers they can be led into the most radical expe-rimentation or the tenderest revelation. I have again and again been astounded by students having to explain to me original effects, connections they tried for, which were too delicate, too modestly put, to register (to me). The complexity of their thought will often get in the way of their expressiveness. When one can midwife such effects, work is going well.

Students come more immediately to a sense of empathy with personality than with ideas. It's more real for them; ideas just don't exist, even for adults, unless identified with something tangible. Often this begins with a person, a teacher figure, and then may spread, if the person is modest enough to ease out of the picture, into such things as the rhythm of one's statement, which leads to poetry.

Once the students have begun writing out of their own resources—and the nature of the exercises forces either that or nothing—they have begun concurrently to be on their own, to have to empathize with themselves, to find in what is just theirs, uniquely and universally, liveliness struggling into speech.

"REAL-LIFE" PIECES

One day I looked out the window and I saw pigeons flying round and round. I sat down and started to stare. As my mind blurred the pigeons began to look like stars as the sky turns gray and gloomy. As they turned from the left and turned from the right, they looked like different color dots in the sky. Soon I began to feel like I was whirling around in the sky just like the pigeons were doing.
—*Albert Negron, 6th*

A leaf fell off a tree. I was looking at it coming down. When it reached the ground it was lost because there were so many. But I had found it because it was the only green leaf with white tiny veins on it. All of a sudden I felt as if I were in the world of leaves and trees. Then I thought there was no city or nothing, just leaves and trees.
—*Carmen Alvarez, 6th*

Empathy triggers, respectively, expansion and focus.

ABOUT POETRY

Poetry is looking at the boat floating on the water and feeling seasick.
—*Wilmer Melendez, 5th*

Empathy ain't just peaches and cream.

Poetry is like a bird
flying from side to side.
It feels like a person without
a mind. But with *your* mind,
and the bird's too....
—*Marilyn Lopez, 6th*

Makes the distinction between flight and progress, shows poetry as mindless but personal (meaning, I suppose, intuitive). It's scary and limited, but glorious, to think of occupying a bird's mind. But with empathy you *can* do a little of this, and then return to your own mind with gifts from out there.

Chapter XVI

OTHER METHODS

"1. Look at that pigeon."

This chapter is devoted to other forms and devices.

13 WAYS OF LOOKING

Wallace Stevens' "13 Ways of Looking at a Blackbird" has often been used by writing teachers to stimulate a multifaceted approach and the associative freedoms that go with it.

13 WAYS OF LOOKING AT A PIGEON

1. Look at that pigeon.
2. Man, it looks crazy.
3. Oh oh, it laid an egg on my head.
4. Holy Cow! Yolk! Yuck!
5. Might as well cook it.
6. Man, it sure stinks. I forgot to wash this pan.
7. Tastes good.
8. Tastes nasty.
9. I burned my finger!
10. I feel like shooting a bird today, but no way.
11. But I can't because I am in a hut.
12. You know something? Holy cow, a thunderstorm!
13. Holy Moley! My whole floor's wet!
   —David Vigo, 2nd

The poet achieves a wild humor immediately, mainly through the combination of numbering and the extreme informality of the items. The first line especially is perfect that way.

7 WAYS TO LOOK AT A LION

1. Upside-down.
2. Around.
3. Straight.
4. Backwards.
5. Forwards.
6. Sideways.
7. Inside-out.
   —*Michael Gonzalez, 2nd*

Number 1 is great. Numbers 2, 3, and 6 are delicious in progression, and then the understatement or minimalism of presentation almost lets the climax, number 7, slip by. Again, that the form conceals a story gives the story additional power.

ALTERED POEMS

A playful ice-breaker, or introduction to surreal juxtapositions, or shot of irreverence, if such seems needed, is the Altered Poem. In the case at hand, Blake's "The Sick Rose" (see Appendix) was subjected to change—nouns replaced by other nouns, verbs by other verbs, etc.—in the key spots, just for fun.

THE CRAZY PEANUT

O peanut, you are nuts,
The invisible chicken
That eats in the shoe,
In the screaming salt,

Has ice-creamed your bed
Of roast beef soup,
And his dark secret jello
Does your nose destroy.
   —*Class collaboration, 1st-2nd*

By working with a whole class, serving as blackboard secretary with editorial powers, you can bring out fine degrees of moderation. The class will immediately be involved in each detailed decision with a rush of subtle concern for tone. Even within the wild goofiness of the above example, care in common was exerted toward a certain restraint.

NUMBERS POEMS

A device especially for very young students is the Numbers poem. Using the basic 0 through 9, ask students to call out phrases that come to mind, based on physical resemblance or meanings of the numbers or anything else. Following are two class collaborations.

THE NUMBERS

0—a man who doesn't have a face.
1—a stick without bark on it.
2—a fish hook trying to catch an eagle.
3—a bee.
4—a box on a stick, a flaming match.
5—riding a bike, a happy face, a green monster, a diving board.
6—a tomato, a tornado or a nose (a sneeze).
7—a triangle missing a side, a broken star.
8—a mask or a roller coaster.
9—a ball hitting the wall, a snowball on a stick.
    —2nd grade

This one concentrates on the technique.

NUMBERS TALE

0—A hole in the hat where the cat lives with
1—a tilted dash and a skinny stick. He says
2—"I'm feeling blue, two dots, eyes." There's
3—an eagle with three people watching, a crowd.
4—Me, my friend and more
5—are taking a dive
6—into the whirlpool,
7—then I have to go to Heaven
8—so open the gate
9—so I won't be late—that's fine.
    —K-1st grade

This poem eases the technique into a continuity.

NEVER-HAPPEN POEM

A sentence could never be a pumpkin.
A noun could never be a meaning.
A Kaisha could never be a white.
    —Kaisha White, 5th

Lovely slants off meaning, especially in progression!

WHEN-I-WAS-POEM

When I was a bodega I ate everything.
I ate so much I turned into an
elephant. When I was wind I joined
a gang of wind, and nowadays
we go in a tornado.
When I was a dog I barked my

head off. I barked so much I
turned into a tree.
—*Robert Diaz, 2nd*

Variety of the metamorphoses, and their handling.

LAST-WORDS POEMS

These poems were triggered by William Carlos Williams' "Last Words of My English Grandmother" (see Appendix).

WOODY WOODPECKER

Woody was stumbling in what used to be a forest. When he was young kids had loved him, but it was over. He laughed and faded into the wind of television.
—*Jose Torres, 6th*

Beautifully brief for such perfect pathos. "Laughed" without further notice is exquisite, as is "the wind of television."

PORKY PIG

As I walked into the house I heard a funny noise. I went into his room and saw a paler face than I saw yesterday. I felt his pulse, he was breathing very badly. I was going to give him mouth to mouth resuscitation but I thought, "What if my breath stinks? Or what if someone walks in?" He died one minute afterwards. His last words were, "Th-th-th-that's all, folks."
—*Anonymous, 6th*

The funny noise and paler face help make it real. The considerations regarding mouth-to-mouth resuscitation are just that sort of thing an adult would think about but almost never admit to. Inevitable joke at end can't be denied.

SESTINA

Following is a sestina done collaboratively in one class period on the blackboard. A fortuitous attitude prevailed, i.e., attention on flavor of language and not just getting the story wrapped up.

Today's a special holiday
for King Kong, that special gorilla,
who jumped in the ocean,
took a mermaid and went up the mountain.
He heard the soft music
that reminded him of a black color.

The mountain was a blend of many colors
that reminded him of a holiday.
He growled the soft music,
what a famous gorilla!
He fell off the mountain
and rolled into the middle of the ocean.

Floating in the ocean,
they splashed the blue color
onto the snowy mountain,
sprinkles of joy on a holiday,
on the beautiful day of gorilla.
They floated to the beat of the music.

Roaring and singing the music,
swimming in the shining cold ocean,
the tender gorilla
with the fresh brown and black colors
covering his skin like a holiday,
floating and watching the mountain...

Taller than the ivory mountain,
with his ear in the wind's music,
jumping around inside the holiday,
stronger than the radiant ocean,
bursting with color,
went the sorrow of King Kong the gorilla.

Out of the ocean came the gorilla,
coming back to the mountain,
and the mountain changed color
as it changed the music.
He let the mermaid float back into the ocean;
that was the end of the holiday.

The holiday of a magic gorilla
may flash and crash between ocean and mountain,
crash of soft music, flash of fresh color.
  —*5th-6th grade*

HAIKU

Haiku can be done with various degrees of adherence to "the rules." I've usually asked for the 5-7-5 syllable count but I'd recommend free three-or-so liners (it's O.K. if they become "short poems" instead of "haiku") for a group long worked with. From the start, however, I've abjured the mention-a-season needs of Japanese tradition and let the poems be American (anything).

D-d-don't stop, just
get on the half haiku, don't
stop the syllables!
—*Kaisha White, 5th*

Sparkling, clever play with the haiku structure.

You don't have to make
your bed, because sooner or
later you'll be dead.
—*Marc Santiago, 7th*

Neat as a skeleton rhyme-flow.

CRASH! BOOM! WHAM! SMACK! BANG!
They sure don't make cereals
like they used to do.
—*Robert Rivera, 7th*

The "do" seems to be padding, but it's pretty good padding.

I have a cousin,
his name is Jimmy Nolan.
I love him so much.
—*Lanette Ware, 8th*

The jump from naming to emotion is quick and effective.

In the shady lane
the people of the Netherlands
talk about the poems.
—*Michael Gonzalez, 2nd*

The sober sound holds back awhile the impact of the realization that this is a highly unexpectable vision.

The pretty blue sky
doesn't move when clouds pass by.
It looks so unreal.
—*Adrienne Owens, 6th*

The implication that everything real moves is good and may remind the reader of Heraclitus' "Everything flows."

Reincarnation,
it could be various things
like rainbows fading.
—*Maurice Melendez, 7th*

Virtuoso touch, having the first line one five-syllable word. Helps make it seem more solid, self-contained. That, the sound, and the tight tone balance the extravagance of the fading rainbows image, which broadens the reader's thoughts of what can reincarnate to what.

WORD-CHAIN POEMS

A device of my invention (which I later learned had also been invented by the poet Dick Gallup) is the word-chain poem, born from my penchant for a light lead from line to line. The rule is to repeat one word from line 1 in line 2, repeat another word from line 2 in line 3, etc. The words can be placed anywhere within the line. Resulting poems often violate the rules, but I've left them as composed, letting the students determine their own degrees of that continuity.

When the sun goes down
the sun will fall asleep.
And when the sun sleeps he's dreaming about the world.
And when the sun sleeps, the people
start dreaming, and the light
starts when we need it.
And in the morning the light starts too.
The eggs start cooking
when the lady starts smiling.
　　　—Anonymous, 5th

Starts beautiful and gets better. Last two lines are terrific in their correspondence to shapes and functions already established.

The boy in the corner looks very white.
The sun is very hot.
But the sun shines on everyone but him.
The boy is very white.
He has a paper in his hand and it is the same color as his face.
He is white because when he was in his mother's stomach
His mother drank a little bit of Clorox.
　　　—Shirelle Santiago, 7th

Ghostly scene sets up punchline.

　　　　　　　　　　There was once a blind old man,
he was blind as a bat.
He looked in the mirror and didn't see nothing.
And he looked out the window and saw the sun on his face.
And his wife made him something to eat
And as he picked up the spoon and took some soup
He forgot that he didn't have a mouth.
　　　—Diane Toles, 7th

Crazy, mean, and downhome.

The sun went down in the city.
Then the city went down and
the sun went up.
I came rolling after.
　　　—Louis Hiciano, 6th

This reminds me of the hornpipe, a sailor's dance with frisky ups and downs and skitterings about.

> There was a cat in the street once.
> He was a dirty cat,
> dirty as the street.
> The street was full of cats,
> but I liked that one.
> And then I took him home and cleaned him
> and that's the end of that.
> —*Jose Garcia, 5th*

Line 4 has a peculiar property of multiplying the focus, just for a second. Last line excellently brings a rhyme home rather distantly, mainly through repetition of both "cat" and "that."

WRITING WHAT YOU HEAR

Another device is to ask the students to write what they hear. I've found that variety may be stimulated by simply putting "Write down what you hear" on the blackboard, without further explanation. One can contribute noises then, as the students write, little yodels, scratches, and pings, if one does not draw attention away from the tiny noises that occur even when people are quiet. It's surprising how different kids will have very different takes on what there is to hear, internally as well as externally.

> O, what, yea but what, what you hear, you people, O, hey, what, merry harry have a little man, tuntun, tun, what you are, ha ha, nut nut, chuck chuck, snap. What a woman had i fuu had i fuu, bum bum, mama, hay guchu cachu ribbit haam ouuouu ouu meow meow. what a woman, qua qua qua chicken, how old that tan tanta tan. The skeleton Joy Jocelyn what's up. Say somethin. O yo cielito lindo ese lunar que tiene junto a la boca no se lode a nadie que a mi me toca, mariba chut chut chut. Chut the door. Shake the hands.
> —*Lory Guzman, 3rd*

Lory's piece is mainly heard inside the head. It comes close to recording instant-by-instant mind function, before things are rationally selected and arranged. Being in tune with the subconscious like this, even if chaotically, is good practice and exciting in itself.

EXTRACT POEMS

Complex devices for making poems can, for one thing, help break up the sense of burden the solitary poetic ego tends to carry. One such device I have developed is to have the students freewrite for, say, a minute and a half. First I give them examples to encourage them to be wildly associative (if they like), then ask them to extract and list vertically nine words from what they've writ-ten. Then I ask them to pair these with a prefabricated (by me) list of nine words. The students can then write poems in which those pairs of words ap-pear, line-by-line. Some of the words they have to work with will thus be their own, some shared by the rest of the class.

> A feather is a perfect thing.
> It's like a ballerina's head drifting
> out to sea, jumping over
> waves more than three times her size.
> The sea swallows her up and now the air is clear.
> Slowly she disappears, to the
> bottom of the sea, thinking about something, and
> then suddenly she's afraid.
> Her words are a whisper, toward the Twilight Zone.
> —*Leara Bowles, 6th*

In this poem Leara has managed to "make sense" while retaining plenty of the wild, dreamlike associations forced by the words she had to work into the lines.

> Rhythm in which sound makes pleasure or myth. A myth in which makes a glare of a dog or a human being. A beard in which you can jump and get swallowed. A sincere place to live. A system that will snare in the sunset. A healthy person in whom will ride a bike in the sky.
> —*John Lamboy, 6th*

The experimental side of the venture emerges strongly here. The piece sounds "crazy" but has the air of genuine inner vision. The connections seem more originally imaginative than most.

> Life is not always perfect. It has crazy things running in your head. Nutty things, things that jump, and lonely things are the three kinds of things in my head. There are happy things in the air at times, and weird things that leave you at a slow pace. A thing like this can make you think about it. You're caught short and afraid in your mind. This crap is what bothers me as it pushes me toward a breakdown.
> —*Jose Torres, 6th*

The tone is sensible, but the student has been inspired to talk *about* disturbing thoughts. The "three kinds of things" in his head and such phrases as "weird things that leave you at a slow pace" have poetic impact.

APRIL FOOLS

In season, April Fools will do fine. I simply ask the students to proclaim im-possible or at least untrue things to a hypothetical "you." Since this is a writing exercise, it's worthwhile to urge that they up the imaginative force over the usual spider-on-your-shoulder.

> Windows are made of plastic bricks.
> Skin is made from aluminum foil.
> Some pencils are made from dog-brain.
> Lips are made from bubblegum leftover
> and some waffles are made from wrinkled stomachs.
> —*Jose Rivera, 3rd*

> Why does your hair pop out?
> The fruits you eat are going to turn to ants.
> Broccoli is made out of Barry Manilow's hand.
> —*Rafael Concepcion, 3rd*

> Your hair is falling off, your ears are wiggling and your eyes are coming out and your face is cracking up and your shoes are gum.
> My friend Walter the Waterbug is crawling on your head.
> —*Kara Alfonso, 3rd*

PANTOUMS

The pantoum is a Malaysian form involving the repetition of entire lines of the poem. Since the line has to be fresh the second time too, it's a natural lesson in working with context. The second example below was a class collaboration, with me serving as blackboard secretary and editor. Both examples are variations on the pantoum form.

> Near or far doesn't mind,
> just be friends
> to the end of the earth
> where angels awake to see you.

> Just be friends,
> even if you go to the moon
> where angels awake to see you
> and comfort you.

> Even if you go to the moon,
> make more friends, sing
> and comfort yourself
> while you enjoy your days and nights.

> Make more friends, sing,
> even if they are different, but
> while you enjoy your days and nights
> near or far doesn't mind.
> —*Shunda Campbell, 5th*

A TRIP THROUGH THE DARK BLUE SEA

A ship sails around the sea
Rapidly in dark blue waters,
Through Europe to Asia and back to me,
Firecrackers bursting in the sky.

Rapidly in dark blue waters
The ship sails into the harbor;
Firecrackers bursting in the sky
Light up the beautiful sea.

The ship sails into the harbor.
The wind blows hard, it's coming to me.
Lighting up the beautiful sea,
People are looking for their families.

The wind blows hard, it's coming to me
To tell of great adventures.
People are looking for their families;
Everyone's singing and dancing.
      —4th grade

CAPTURED TALK

I assigned students to record snatches of talk in the course of their daily lives
and to string them together as pieces of "found poetry."

Good morning America this is
WNBC radio! Good evening this is
You Asked For It! Let's start
with the sword-swallower. We'll
be back with more 11 Alive after
these messages. Come on, you're
coming with me! Operator, get
me the police. Stick 'em up,
this is a holdup! When it's
time to relax, one beer stands
clear. Miller Beer. Police!
Police! He took my purse. You
want to go to the circus. Our
next incredible story is about a
15-year-old boy with no hands.
Scooby Dooby Doo, where are you,
pretending you got a fever. You
count on me 'cause I can see the
way you shake and shiver.
      —Anonymous, 4th

BUS TALK

Hi, how are you?
This is my stop.
Where are you going?
Give me your hand.
Hey, there's the fish market.
Can I have a transfer?
Look, that's Brooke Shields.
What time is it?
Mommy, how many more stops?
Let's see Lucy.
Mommy, I have to go to the
  bathroom.
    Last Stop.
    Everybody off!
      —*Monique Cuevas, 4th*

Bananas!
where did you get it!
not sure.
I wouldn't know.
the Brady Bunch.
it's never going to work.
lose weight, one coke is it.
wait and see.
take it easy.
Carter.
that's for Mom!
rated R.
it's gonna take a miracle.
roll-a-matic.
satisfaction guaranteed.
Camay all over.
movie nine.
Craftmatic Bed.
you lied!
just once.
the fat one?
my Communion.
the pigeons.
it's cold!
in church.
I did not!
why did it happen?
that'll be the day!
I did not!
I remember it.
let's get physical!
Ivory soap.

why not?
create a villain.
Mr. Zzzzzzzuliani.
Nestle's Quik.
Kool-Aid.
that was cold!
unknown record.
you did.
alright, alright!
you will always remember.
I can't let you go.
I can't go for that!
Nut zippers.
no frills.
let me hear your body talk.
have style!
Freshes-up.
mama! delicious.
that's right.
relax.
listen, Son.
Holy Cow!
Oh no! last Sunday?
how did you do it?
because you love him.
where's the money?
one more time.
that was great!
come tomorrow.
that means a lot.
take your time.
BYE!!!!!
— *Maritza Osorio, 6th*

Framing these bits of speech as lines of a poem brings out their humor and energy, especially jammed as they are into a series that makes no pretense at "sense" and thereby encourages the hearer to concentrate on the flavor of the language.

MAKING DEFINITIONS AND ALPHABETRAX

Another small exercise of the icebreaker type, especially for loosening up the imagination, goes like this: from the dictionary select a word unknown to the class and ask them to make up their own definitions for it. With proper lead-in and good examples you'll get a startling potpourri of imaginative results, from "the moment before bone implosion" to "a cloud that glows in the dark." You can follow this, within one class period, with another brief imagination exercise, such as Alphabetrax (invented by Alison Dale), in which the students are asked to make up trios of words using their initials. The words can "make sense," like "Just A Curlyhead," or not, like "Jupiter Asparagus Crackup." Or you can follow the dictionary game by requesting that they take one of their definitions and elaborate it into a poem. Here are two examples of the latter, in each of which the magic of names takes place.

> A praline is a girl's name coming from everywhere. You can hear
> her name coming closer and closer until you go crazy hearing her
> name. Everywhere you go, praline, praline.
> When you go to your mother she says Praline.
> When you go to your father he says Praline.
> When you ask a girl out she says Praline.
> And then you find out you're in the *Praline Zone*.
> —*William Pena, 6th*

> The person is a cloud that glows
> in the dark. It comes from the
> sky and sings through the night.
> Every night I hear the tone, it
> sounds so beautiful that I sing
> with that person. Then that person
> comes out from the sky and
> starts singing the song once more.
> Then I knew who the person was,
> but she's beautiful. She told me
> her name and it was Mosaic. Then
> she sang a song about her name.
> —*Sandra Santiago, 5th*

WORD-ACROSTICS

Another device of my invention is the word-acrostic. Instead of letters going down the left edge forming a word, words (in capital letters) go down, forming a phrase or sentence.

> ONCE I saw a movie.
> UPON my bed was
> A kitten. He was pretty. He had
> TIME to see it too.
> —*Jose Arias, 4th*

Another is a rhyme scheme in which the last word (or syllable) of each line is rhymed *anywhere* within the following line.

One can invent one's own poetic forms, keeping in mind, for classroom use, that the progression from line to line may well be helped by some device but that overprescription should probably be avoided. I have never used cinquains for that reason — more like a crossword puzzle fillout than a poem.

Chapter XVII

CONCLUSION: EVALUATION

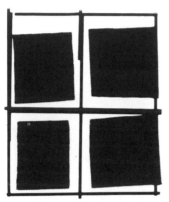

In the course of writing this book I received a letter from its editor, Ron Padgett, which included the following:

"At the risk of pontificating, I want to say that teachers should know that taste in art does exist, that it is variable, that it does change through history, that it is never final, that art is not good without it, that it is maddeningly elusive, that no one has *the* answer but that we can never stop looking for one. They should know that a sense of what's good and beautiful and true in art can be acquired, or at least more of it can be acquired, by experiencing art, both as a passive observer and as a participant. They should know that complacency and immodesty have no place in a person trying to find out what's best about the best in art, and conversely, that one should not be insecure or apologetic about what one does not yet know. In other words, it's 'You go on your nerve' (Frank O'Hara) in evaluating art, but only while giving your nerve a more informed body of information to work with. Ultimately, teachers should know that they must *never* grade their students' poetry, but that they must form value judgments about that poetry, for otherwise they will never be able to do more than give generic encouragement, which does wear thin. Finally, teachers should know that they can and should guide their students' aesthetic sense and values, because peer criticism among students is good only so far as it goes, which in most cases isn't very far."

I agree. One needs to have a delicate line in mind between such modes of statement as "This is a valid poetic doctrine" and "Here's what I feel." And of course that delicate line is, in another sense, a large and varied continent. Evaluation is always tricky. It always verges on the arbitrary, and one should never lose track of one's humility in the face of that. History teaches us that the most exciting works and styles have been misjudged again and again. The length of their misjudgment is virtually a criterion of their worth. We may look back at the condemnation of Donne or Beethoven for being too "rough" and smile, thinking we are now, late twentieth century, beyond such misjudgment, but the critical capacity of any individual or, indeed, any period is *always* limited. Nevertheless, we must evaluate; a proportion of evaluation would seem necessary in the whole atmosphere around art, as a device, or presence, against self-indulgence.

In evaluating children's works, there is a certain superior ease we can fall into which may become too routine. Many pieces are so clearly faulty, and the faults so unambiguously simple, that we can respond with a confident red slash, at a glance. We needn't fear overmuch that we are rejecting a Shakespeare-like body of work. But in the process we may be rejecting instances of tiny Shakespearesque explosions, sometimes buried in material that does not work, sometimes hidden in a style so unpretentious as to lull our perceptions.

Being a poet generally entails a particular body of expertise (from anapests to aesthetic theory). But another, even more powerful, body of expertise exists in poetry, and is shared by nearly everyone—the ability to talk. It is a massively complex skill, honed by everyone for thousands and thousands of hours. Nearly everyone talks, most write, and the material of poetry—language—is used in many *other* highly developed ways. To their specialized adherents, the virtues and delights of critical exposition or song lyrics, oratory or mash notes, glossolalia or physics notations, advertising copy or street-talk may seem to assume primary importance in language, and that poetry thereby faulted that does not mirror those particular fine strengths. Or people may want to assign poetry a limited tone, usually of a familiar romantic flavor, as a relief from "reality."

"The Poet" is a term peculiarly different from "The Painter" or "The Actor." It stands somewhat generically for the Soul of Art and, despite or because of that, has a flip-side connotation of "The Flowery Dolt." In part, this is due to the universal expertise involved. Everybody has an opinion about poetry. Or if they don't, it amounts to an opinion that poetry is irrelevant. The emphasis in most language uses is, or purports to be, on content. Language is believed to be, in an up-front way, just a vehicle for thought and fact. This attitude is perhaps a survival from times when the question of survival loomed so large as to render every consideration pragmatic. People project an expectation of conventional communication onto poetry. But content, as such, is free, hardly a quiver from fact to page, while the airs and exactitudes of language cost the entire person.

Large aspects of the universal verbal expertise are subconscious. People don't realize or give credit to the complexity of their own communications repertoires. We recognize that music can be fully expressive without words, through rhythm, melody, harmonics, counterpoint, dynamics, and tone. But our own speech constantly uses all these—plus the powers of gesture, facial expression, and other emotive factors — to make its points, intended or otherwise. Poetry intensifies, plays with, lets fly, and sometimes patterns these qualities of music that fill speech. A fact can be delicately brought out, a fact can be danced through any guise whatsoever. But since we rely on the convenience of a denotative understanding of language, poetry is easily misunder-stood. Emotion and music outlive ideas.

In prior ages of English-language verse, stricter ideas of pattern dominated. Most poets felt they must master and work within given forms. Refinement of discipline was looked upon by many as poetry's highest formal aim. In retrospect, we find now that the greatest artists were those of *innovative* mastery. Such artists were often, in their own times, considered unpolished. The pendulum swings (or at least the spiral whirls), and nowadays the empha-sis is, more than then, on individualized expression.

One great advantage in the stiff requirements of former times was the mi-nute attention forced by the formal demands. In constructing one's thought ac-cording to rhyme and meter, or the triply alliterative line, one became of neces-sity intimate with the atoms, the nuts and bolts, of the work. In the present aesthetic climate, there are doubtless abuses of the available freedom. Poets scribble, slur over their proper cares. But abuses of poetic doctrine, or its lack, are inevitable in any age. Reams upon reams of empty—but rhymed and iambic —sentiments clog the history of verse. And beyond that are other considera-tions. "Scribbling," writing fast, may evoke spontaneous beauties of revela-tion, energy, even musicality, that a more conscious care would tend to inhibit or express stodgily. And the good poets in any age, any style, will be moved to focus their energy as exactly as words can take. T. S. Eliot said that free verse, by which he meant good free verse, was the most difficult form, since all the responsibilities are the author's; none is already solved in the system.

One thing a system provides is tension. Poets like Alexander Pope developed exquisite skills at keeping to the form and at the same time constant-ly playing with it, violating its dead-average thrust — bottling up their repugnance to boom-de-boom boredom till it was ready to blow up, in the reader's brain. But the possibilities for tension are endless in poetry, in or out of a given structure.

Nevertheless, resistance is still strong to what seem in modern poetry to be violations of tradition. This is also true in the other arts, and in fact in every aspect of modern life. In fact, it has always been true. Resistance toward change is always strong. Nor is this to be automatically deplored. Resistance and movement work together, against each other, to make change tolerable. But in poetry change is of the essence.

●

Writing poetry involves a combination of the ability to talk and the knowledge needed to compose consciously, strengthened by the experience of application, lit up by a "feel" for doing it. In other words, poetic success grows from a shifting complex of qualities ranging from exactitude to a "blind" gift for it. Part solid, part liquid. Reality fantasy. Relaxed concentration. Universal novelty. Immeasurable precision. We tend to barge into this nest of paradoxes, if we barge at all, armed with standards or attitudes and thereby scant one side or another of the total poetry.

An appreciator (which must include "evaluator") of poetry should ideally bring the same intensity to the work as the artist did in making it. Thus we can never relax with a final body of knowledge. No good poetry lives entirely within such knowledge. Nor can we rely solely on the favorable glow of our emotional response, which can degenerate into judgment by how well the piece confirms our philosophy of life, or doesn't upset us, or seems healthy, or reminds us of beautiful thoughts we've had. Of course the reverse can become sentimental too.

The sense of art as emotional salve—for convention *or* rebellion—is a lazy approach, especially dangerous in poetry due to the confusing variety of language's uses. This is not to imply that the language of poetry is special, has nothing to do with the language of exposition, chit-chat, propaganda, and grocery lists. On the contrary, poetry has a deep connection with all language uses. The precision of exposition, the feeling and rhythm of chit-chat, the expressivity of propaganda, and the musical realism of a grocery list are all prime poetic ingredients.

The difference is in purpose. In a sense, poetry *lacks* purpose, so that one is not distracted from taking in all the elements — the musicality, the surprises, the passion, the disguises, the sensitivities to word and world. One gets via the best poets, in detail, a feeling of the closeness of one person to humanity at large *and* a feeling of the breathtaking uniqueness of each. Subjectively this is purpose, but purpose that has been held back from coalescing as such till we are further than usual along the expansion that occurs from every statement as from every pebble dropped in water. Objectively, we are delighted and edified by good poetry, but the edification may be what we couldn't have predicted and the delight outside our run of habits.

So we approach a kid's poem, at best, with the power to gobble up Shakespeare, on one hand, and a readiness to cast away all the power of our knowledge, on the other. No one can do this. It just means that the scope of possible appreciation and evaluation is virtually infinite. I have time and again compromised my penetration into the magic of language in this book, have made do with arbitrary and repetitive reductions. At least, knowing this, I have tried hard not to.

Evaluation and its expression, criticism, have the burden, more thoroughly than creativity does, of forcing insight into the conscious mind. A verbal gesture is less apt to suffice than in a poem. On the other hand, evaluation has the ease of working on something already given. You don't have to give birth to a perfect egg of soul when you make a critical statement. Grammatical corrections (when they don't harm the piece's spirit) and such remarks as "The extra syllable here makes the rhythm awkward" or "Can you think of something more original here?" or "See how the thought falls apart in the fourth line?" or "Here the rhyme takes over and there's nothing else there" may be just fine. It's difficult for criticism to get beyond such details and not risk seeming to criticize the writer's soul, yet the kid feels the lack when no mention is made of the spirit of the piece. One can safely praise any original sense of larger feeling "behind" a young poet's piece. The word "original" is the key; students should be made to realize that they can't just ride the coat-tails of a generalized emotive word. They must build room and justification for such senses out of the details of their own perceptions.

Evaluation in and around the classroom has two faces: what you tell the kid and what you really think (or how you select). These two should be *as closely as possible* the same face. The only difference should be—partly because one doesn't ultimately know for sure and partly as a spur—that what you tell the kid should include encouragement. Often there's no problem: it's "Wow" and why (the latter within prudent limits so the students don't feel they have a prescription to fill and refill). Often you can gently pick out "hits" within an otherwise mediocre poem and draw attention to them. The lack of praise for the unmentioned elements will usually serve as sufficient criticism in these circumstances. If the poem seems inept throughout, there is almost always a way to speak of the spirit of the student's attempt that may encourage the student and yet not compromise your sense of what's good in poetry. Depending on the kid, you can (surprisingly often, especially the more "technical" the criticism is) say harsh things ("This line doesn't work at all") *when* you can balance them with sincere praise of something else about the child's work. Keep in mind that for "sensitive" children ten seconds of criticism has the force of ten minutes of praise.

I stress and approve of originality. I find it basic to poetic worth even in the most traditional forms. Kids tend to have a strong talent for original expression but low confidence in its value. They will generally approach writing with already enough or too much respect for tradition. Not that they will know it that keenly; such knowledge depends on adult or adult-like skill. The recapitulation of traditional form or thought will be their weakest ability. Their respect for tradition will often be so unquestioning as to be no respect at all, but rather the forced amiability of pleasing authority. But just beneath the surface of their institutional habits of speech will lie founts of linguistic initiative, human in general and young in particular. This is the first thing to be encouraged. If the spirit doesn't come first, very little will come at all. Those who continue writing, as a personal interest, will in due time have to face the impersonality that must be assimilated for it. Those who don't continue will at least have experienced some flashes of feeling that may, in small ways, vivify their lives, including their approach to other subjects in school.

But the tricky thing is that originality and precision are one; that is, they meet in their very substance, like the sides of a coin. Student writers and others may be seduced by semblances of these two qualities that are really evidences of stopping too soon in the search for them. E.g., "I chopped off the million green heads of the drooling giant woodchuck with my sword of light" is not originally imaginative, nor is "The beautiful flowers spring/ In Spring and quietly sing" profoundly precise. Each one makes too easy a bargain with the common image of the quality involved. The word that looms is "cliché." But even here we cannot operate solely on principle. Clichés may be, in perspective, wonderful in poetry. Children perceive clichés very keenly but in a different light than educated adults. At best, children use them more boldly than we do, yet manage to throw them into contexts they've never had before. In which case they're no longer clichés.

The realities of teaching may necessitate other—what one might want to call aesthetically political—responses. In high school, for example, many students have achieved sophistication enough to argue what they want and make it seem as if it comes from objective theory. Chiefly this takes the form of a regard for "soul" so pure and incandescent that your demand for details seems crass and unworthy. Then this attitude frequently rebounds to extremes of academic symbolism, or to cynical dodges, avoiding poetry. Such matters can be pretty easily argued out, and even be the vehicles through which valuable points of the art arrive in class. The chief danger is that debate itself may assume too strong an emphasis in the dynamics of poetry. A classroom bull-session can be the least poetry-like function imaginable, intellection and ego problems assuming all. And precious time, which is always squeezed anyway, lost. Discussion, which is needed to some degree, has a much greater coefficient of expansion than poetry itself in class. I recommend an alert economy in monitoring argument (as opposed to revelation—if a student starts telling a dream it may be just the thing) and a tough-minded spotlighting of the good stuff.

One weakness—though at the same time a phase so common as to be almost necessary—of high school writing is the uncritical "trying out" of whatever the student can do. Students with a large vocabulary and a frustrated sense of self-expression are likely to show off to such extremes as they can carry it. One knows how to evaluate this sort of excess—it is so close to adult sensibility (unlike many of the peculiarities of the younger kids' writings)—but in expressing one's criticism it is difficult to avoid seeming too negative, or too simplemindedly or soullessly Hemingwayesque ("Cut this"). One finds oneself almost grammarian-wise plumping for the tenets of "good writing." I think an approach that will work in such cases is to take examples of good writing that are apparently "wild"—authors such as Céline, Henry Miller, Whitman, Kerouac, Baraka, Stein, and Ginsberg—and show, via detailed focus, how every syllable has at least a musical or emotional logic, and then apply the same focus to the student writing. In the process one can point to the inevitable "hits" or evidences of spirit and leaven the lesson with encouragement.

●

In some cases we move about first and then discover what we're looking for. The thing looked for may be, in effect, a form to sustain personal movement. My boyhood passion was birdwatching, to which I was introduced at age eleven while walking in the woods with a boy named Sam Keen. Sam pointed to a bird with a dark back and bright orange underneath and asked me what it was. "A robin," I said. "It's a towhee," said Sam a little scornfully and I suddenly realized: there are a lot of things out there, differing and resembling.

That same year I read Poe's "The Raven." This was my only vivid experience with poetry until I was grown.

To watch birds you go out of the ordinary, to special places. You become quiet and alert. With luck and care you see colorful and musical things that fly about. You zero in on details while not forgetting larger impressions.

In reading or writing poetry, the special place may be inside the head and the colorful, musical, "flying" things may be words, phrases, and images, but the whole pursuit can be seen as parallel to watching birds.

As a boy in Illinois woods, I once climbed toward a red-tailed hawk's nest. My two friends, with whom I did some falconry, waited below. In early spring we would locate all the hawks' nests in several miles of woods, then keep track of them and eventually take a nestling or two to train for hunting. We loved the birds and followed the rules, though we broke the law. This particular nest contained freshly hatched young and I was just checking. As I climbed, urgent cries of the unseen mother circled the tree. Then suddenly she was above and dived at me. She hit my back with claws curled to fists, as a peregrine falcon knocks ducks out of the sky. I turned right around and returned to earth. And we three hiked on.

At Wolf Road Bridge, on branches that ran up right to where I was standing, I saw the only two Blackburnian warblers of my childhood. This bird is small, usually energetically chasing bugs in high green leaves, only passes through temperate America. Its color is the most brilliant I know, head and breast of bright black and orange. Twenty years later I wrote this stanza, of the kind called "royal" but in tetrameter:

> There's something strange about the name
> Of the small Blackburnian warbler. Who
> Have seen the head and breast of flame
> Boldly laced with ebony through
> The light green leaves of May eschew
> A man called Blackburn, swiftly turning
> Back to thought of blackness and burning.

One winter, years ago, in the peculiar week between Christmas and New Year's, I wrote, contrary to my poetic plans, a series of ninety-one short poems about a mythical blue heron. It's still my favorite piece of my own.

Each poet will have his or her own stories and incidents that seem to have spurred particular rides, and the views that came with them. The hawk pounding me on the back made palpable what I'd only looked at before. I kept on climbing trees. The warblers were a focus of beauty, close up. From boyhood blue herons I made my own story, which seemed like it arose of its own accord.

My memory of poetry at school is faded photographs of Longfellow, and a language that didn't reach me. I wrote my first poem at age twenty-three, stationed in Libya, almost from a process of elimination of things I could do and of things I could do that day. What made me try it a second and third time was the sense of discovery. I found that I wasn't just writing what I knew, identifying robins, but that the movement through the poem brought variations and surprises. I felt that there was no end to it.

I wish I had started writing earlier. I also wish someone had been there, on occasion, to speak in detail of what I was doing. I know it would have been all too easy for injudicious criticism to depersonalize, perhaps for life, what writing I might have done. But poetry has to be tested in the world, in good time. The moment eye or ear takes it in, the process has begun.

APPENDIX

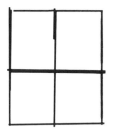

PLEASURES

I like to find
what's not found
at once, but lies

within something of another nature,
in repose, distinct.
Gull feathers of glass, hidden

in white pulp: the bones of squid
which I pull out and lay
blade by blade on the draining board —

tapered as if for swiftness, to pierce
the heart, but fragile, substance
belying design.   Or a fruit, *mamey*,

cased in rough brown peel, the flesh
rose-amber, and the seed:
the seed a stone of wood, carved and

polished, walnut-colored, formed
like a brazilnut, but large,
large enough to fill
the hungry palm of a hand.

I like the juicy stem of grass that grows
within the coarser leaf folded round,
and the butteryellow glow
in the narrow flute from which the morning-glory
opens blue and cool on a hot morning.
                   —*Denise Levertov*

CROSSING

STOP   LOOK   LISTEN
as gate stripes swing down,
count the cars hauling distance
upgrade through town:
warning whistle, bellclang,
engine eating steam,
engineer waving,
a fast-freight dream:
B&M boxcar,
boxcar again,
Frisco gondola,
eight-nine-ten,
Erie and Wabash,
Seabord, U.P.,
Pennsy tankcar,
twenty-two, three,
Phoebe Snow, B&O,
thirty-four, five
Santa Fe cattle
shipped alive,
red cars, yellow cars,
orange cars, black,
Youngstown steel
down to Mobile
on Rock Island track,
fifty-nine, sixty,
hoppers of coke,
Anaconda copper,
hotbox smoke,
eighty-eight,
red-ball freight,
Rio Grande,
Nickel Plate,
Hiawatha,
Lackawanna,
rolling fast
and loose,
ninety-seven,
coal car
boxcar,
CABOOSE!
    —Philip Booth

THE SICK ROSE

O Rose, thou art sick,
The invisible worm
That flies in the night
In the howling storm

Has found out thy bed
Of crimson joy,
And his dark secret love
Does thy life destroy.
　　　　　—*William Blake*

HAY FOR THE HORSES

He had driven half the night
From far down San Joaquin
Through Mariposa, up the
Dangerous mountain roads,
And pulled in at eight a.m.
With his big truckload of hay
　　　　　behind the barn.
With winch and ropes and hooks
We stacked the bales up clean
To splintery redwood rafters
High in the dark, flecks of alfalfa
Whirling through shingle-cracks of light,
Itch of haydust in the
　　　　　sweaty shirt and shoes.
At lunchtime under Black oak
Out in the hot corral,
—The old mare nosing lunchpails,
Grasshoppers crackling in the weeds—
'I'm sixty-eight,' he said,
'I first bucked hay when I was seventeen.
I thought, that day I started,
I sure would hate to do this all my life.
And dammit, that's just what
I've gone and done.'
　　　　　—*Gary Snyder*

TOO BLUE

I got those sad old weary blues.
I don't know where to turn.
I don't know where to go.
Nobody cares about you
When you sink so low.

What shall I do?
What shall I say?
Shall I take a gun and
Put myself away?

I wonder if
One bullet would do?
Hard as my head is,
It would probably take two.

But I ain't got
Neither bullet nor gun—
And I'm too blue
To look for one.
   —*Langston Hughes*

NANTUCKET

Flowers through the window
lavender and yellow

changed by white curtains—
Smell of cleanliness—

Sunshine of late afternoon—
On the glass tray

a glass pitcher, the tumbler
turned down, by which

a key is lying—And the
immaculate white bed
   —*William Carlos Williams*

THE LAST WORDS OF MY ENGLISH GRANDMOTHER

1920

There were some dirty plates
and a glass of milk
beside her on a small table
near the rank, disheveled bed—

Wrinkled and nearly blind
she lay and snored
rousing with anger in her tones
to cry for food,

Gimme something to eat—
They're starving me—
I'm all right—I won't go
to the hospital. No, no, no

Give me something to eat!
Let me take you
to the hospital, I said
and after you are well

you can do as you please.
She smiled, Yes
you do what you please first
then I can do what I please—

Oh, oh, oh! she cried
as the ambulance men lifted
her to the stretcher—
Is this what you call

making me comfortable?
By now her mind was clear—
Oh you think you're smart
you young people,

she said, but I'll tell you
you don't know anything.
Then we started.
On the way

we passed a long row
of elms, she looked at them
awhile out of
the ambulance window and said,

What are all those
fuzzy looking things out there?
Trees? Well, I'm tired
of them and rolled her head away.
—*William Carlos Williams*

THIS IS JUST TO SAY

I have eaten
the plums
that were in
the icebox

and which
you were probably
saving
for breakfast

forgive me
they were delicious
so sweet
and so cold.
—*William Carlos Williams*